ALSO BY RALPH FLETCHER:

MARSHFIELD DREAMS

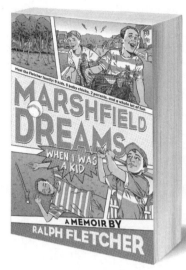

"Written with sagacious eloquence and gentle humor, this work stands strong in the ranks of authors' memoirs and autobiographies."
—*School Library Journal*

"Boisterously good times."
—*Booklist*

"Charming. . . . Sensitive glimpses of a close-knit, traditional family."
—*VOYA*

"This scrapbook of family moments is an amusing, charming and heartwarming memoir. A snapshot of small-world life that will open readers' eyes to the bonds of a peerless time and simpler lifestyle."
—*Kirkus Reviews*

GUY WRITE

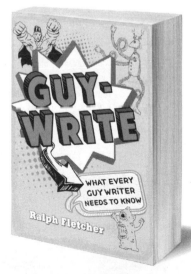

A Tri-State Review Committee Book of Note

"Important reading for teachers as well as budding guy writers."
—*BCCB*

"Encouragement and instructive pointers in a package guy writers will enjoy."
—*Kirkus Reviews*

"A good guide for anyone with a penchant for storytelling, but especially those who trade in 'spoofs, humor, sports, blood, farts [and] giant monsters tearing down the city.'"
—*Booklist*

Tommy and Jimmy

MARSHFIELD
MEMORIES

Me and Carolyn

RALPH FLETCHER

MARSHFIELD MEMORIES

More Stories About Growing Up

Christy Ottaviano Books

HENRY HOLT AND COMPANY
NEW YORK

Henry Holt and Company, *Publishers since 1866*
Henry Holt® is a registered trademark of Macmillan Publishing Group, LLC
175 Fifth Avenue, New York, NY 10010
mackids.com

Library of Congress Cataloging-in-Publication Data
Names: Fletcher, Ralph J., author.
Title: Marshfield Memories : more stories about growing up / Ralph Fletcher.
Description: First edition. | New York, New York : Christy Ottaviano Books/Henry Holt
  and Company, 2018. | Sequel to: Marshfield Dreams.
Identifiers: LCCN 2018004256 | ISBN 9781627795241 (hardcover)
Subjects: LCSH: Fletcher, Ralph J.—Childhood and youth—Juvenile literature. |
  Fletcher, Ralph J.—Homes and haunts—Massachusetts—Marshfield—Juvenile
  literature. | Authors, American—20th century—Biography—Juvenile literature. |
  Marshfield (Mass.)—Social life and customs—Juvenile literature.
Classification: LCC PS3556.L523 I6 2018 | DDC 811/.54—dc23
LC record available at https://lccn.loc.gov/2018004256

Our books may be purchased in bulk for promotional, educational, or business
use. Please contact your local bookseller or the Macmillan Corporate
and Premium Sales Department at (800) 221-7945 ext. 5442 or by e-mail at
MacmillanSpecialMarkets@macmillan.com.

First edition, 2018 / Designed by Rebecca Syracuse

Printed in the United States of America by LSC Communications, Harrisonburg,
Virginia

10 9 8 7 6 5 4 3 2 1

Dad

FOR MY FATHER,
RALPH JOSEPH FLETCHER
1929–2017

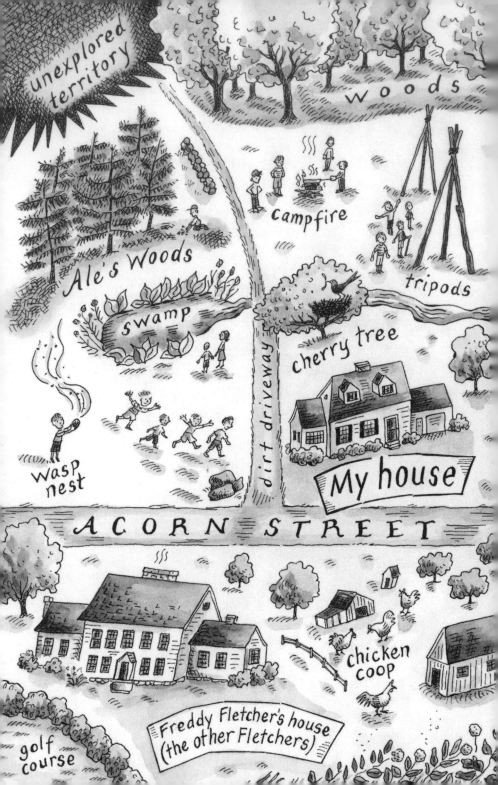

frogs and mud!

Necco

Scouts

birch trees

Marshfield Fair

small stream

Marbles

Andy Hunt's house

Ruben Gonsalves's school bus

mushrooms

Clamming

field

Steve Fishman's house

Johnny

MARSHFIELD
MEMORIES

Me

Introduction

OPEN THE FIRST page of *The Hobbit* by J. R. R. Tolkien. Open any of the three books in the Lord of the Rings trilogy. The first thing you see is a map of Middle-earth, a land of enchantment inhabited by elves, dwarves, orcs, and hobbits. The map shows the names of cities that were home to great battles and epic quests. These cities may be fictional, but they ring in our imaginations like real places we have been.

Well, Marshfield was my Middle-earth. The woods, streams, swamps, and beaches of Marshfield were my Gondor, Lothlórien, the Shire. That's why this book, like my first memoir, *Marshfield Dreams: When I Was a Kid,* begins with a map of the neighborhood where I grew up. For me, looking at this map conjures the magic of that place. I feel lucky and grateful to have had Marshfield as my childhood home. And unlike Middle-earth, Marshfield is a place you can actually visit.

If you look closely at the cross section of a tree trunk, you can see a series of rings that get smaller and smaller. The outside rings are most recent; the inner rings hark back to when the tree was young and just beginning its life. People are like that too. As we age we create similar rings inside of us. The mysteries, triumphs, sorrows, intense loves, and heartbreaks from childhood "ring" through our lives forever.

You never really leave your childhood behind. I am an adult now, but the boy in this book still lives inside me. Right this very minute he's racing down the forest paths of Ale's Woods with Andy

Hunt and Steve Fishman, followed by my brothers Jimmy and Tommy, all of us dodging rocks and roots, whooping and hollering, excited about gathering the neighborhood gang for a huge game of Capture the Flag, Hide-and-Seek, or War.

My lifeblood ran through *Marshfield Dreams*, and it runs through this book as well. When I look at the map, when I dig down beneath the soft carpet of pine needles in Ale's Woods, I know that my most important stories start right here.

—RALPH FLETCHER

Dad

Buffalo

GRANDMA MADE STRAWBERRY shortcake the exact same way Mom made it, so why did Grandma's taste different? The biscuits and whipped cream were the same, but the strawberries in Grandma Annie's dessert left an odd tang on my tongue. I was too polite to mention it, though when I was ten, it really made me wonder. I considered it one of the great mysteries of the world.

Then one night, just before I fell asleep, it hit

me—Grandma Annie sliced the strawberries on her old cutting board. Over the years, she had cut count-less cloves of garlic on the same wooden board. That garlicky taste must have bled into the wood and stained the flavor of the strawberries. Mystery solved.

As I got older, I learned that a similar kind of staining could happen with words. You'd have a regular word, but over time its original meaning could change in an unexpected way. Take the word *buffalo*.

There were eight kids in our family—Ralph (that's me), Jimmy, Lainie, Tommy, Bobby, Johnny, Joey, Kathy—and I was the oldest. The kids in our family called Dad's white bathrobe his buffalo, though I'm not sure how it got that name. Maybe it was because the shaggy robe resembled one of those impressive beasts. Or maybe it was because my father traveled a lot as a book salesman, moving around the country the way buffalo once roamed the western plains. But it's probably simpler than that—most likely one of my siblings called the robe *buffalo*, and the name stuck.

On Sunday night, Dad loaded up his car with boxes of books and left for another business trip. By midweek we would start pestering Mom.

"When's Dad coming home?"

"Friday. I already told you."

After supper, if we had finished our homework, Mom let us watch an hour of TV.

"Could we get out Dad's buffalo?" Elaine (or Lainie, as we called her) asked wistfully.

Mom put her hands on her hips. "Well . . ."

"Please?" Lainie begged. "Just for a little while?"

Mom sighed.

Lainie, Jimmy, Tommy, and I raced upstairs to our parents' bedroom. The buffalo always hung on a particular hook in the closet. We jostled each other to see which of us could pull it down and drag it to the living room. Then we wrapped it around us while we watched TV. The buffalo was big enough to envelop three or even four kids in its shaggy warmth.

Beyond its warmth and softness, the most wonderful thing about that buffalo was the way it soaked up Dad's smell, his essence. I sat there, surrounded by his comforting scent, and discovered that if I closed my eyes and breathed in the smell, I could almost believe he was holding me in his strong arms.

For me, the word *buffalo* is changed, stained like the berries in Grandma Annie's strawberry short-cake. The word makes me think of the mighty beasts that thundered across the Great Plains until they were almost wiped out by white settlers. But *buffalo* has another, more personal meaning that's connected to my father. It reminds me of missing him all those nights when he was away on business trips, as well as the comfort and security I felt when he finally came home.

Jimmy with Kathy

Soggy Eyes

"Spring cleaning!" Dad announced at breakfast. "Mom and I are going to clean the garage."

"O-kay," I said carefully.

"All helpers are welcome," he added.

Inwardly, I groaned. It was exactly the sort of project I always got roped into. But today I was lucky; Dad cut me loose and told me to go play. I grabbed my jacket, laced up my sneakers, and hurried outside before he could change his mind.

The backyard was deserted. I looked over at Andy Hunt's house, but there was nothing stirring there, either. At the edge of the woods I glimpsed a red coat—my sister Lainie standing with my brothers, not far from the swamp. I ran over to join them.

It was late March. Technically spring had arrived, but it must have forgotten to tell the air because there was still a nasty bite. Bright sunlight bathed half of the swamp; the other half was swaddled in shadow. I could see water glistening on the sunny part, but the shadowy section was still crusted over with a layer of ice about a quarter inch thick. Tom and Bob began stomping on the ice, making crunching sounds, as if trying to free the pond from the tyranny of winter. Johnny, who was four, hesitated for a second before he started doing it too.

"Careful," Lainie warned.

I stood there frowning, watching my brothers do their demented dance—*STOMP, STOMP, STOMP*—on the thin ice.

"You're going to get muddy," I muttered.

Jimmy smiled. "So what?"

"Hey, look!" Lainie cried.

At first I couldn't see what she was pointing at. An arrowhead, maybe? I knew for a fact Native Americans had wandered through these woods only a few hundred years ago. But then my eyes detected two little orbs—a pair of soggy eyes—floating just above the surface of the water.

Bobby grinned. "Froggies!"

Jimmy didn't waste any time. He squatted down, and his arm darted forward—*splash!* When he pulled it back I could see that he had grabbed one. The critter squirmed, panicked, trying with all its might to break out of Jimmy's grip. But Jimmy wasn't eager to let go.

"Get a bucket," he ordered.

That was just like Jimmy, to start barking orders and expect everyone to jump to his demands.

"I'll go," Tommy cried, and took off, heading in the direction of our house.

Lainie leaned forward, studying the frog in Jimmy's hand. She squinted up at him.

"What are you going to do with it?"

"Keep it," Jimmy replied. "Obviously."

He squatted down again. His arm leapt forward—*bang!*—he had snatched another one. Now he had frogs clasped in both hands. When Tommy returned, Jimmy plopped them into the plastic bucket.

Bobby caught one next. He grinned at me, his eyes bright and sparkly. "It's easy!"

"Yeah, they're pretty sluggish," Jimmy muttered. "I think they're still waking up."

Jimmy caught a few more. Tommy and Bobby captured frogs at the exact same moment and added their catch to the bucket.

"That's eight," Jimmy yelled. "C'mon, Ralphie. There's a ton in here!"

I felt myself holding back like I often did, but this time for some reason my resistance melted away. Maybe the other kids' excitement infected me, because catching a frog suddenly became THE most important thing in the world. I spotted one and slowly crouched, balancing myself on a flat log. I lunged, but the frog chose that exact moment to jump away, so I only got his right foot. He attempted to escape, but I held on and wrapped him in my hands, trying not to squeeze too tight. The critter felt funny in my grip—all muscle and soft bones—slimy but surprisingly soft.

"I see another one!" Lainie cried.

"Grab it," Jimmy told her.

She made a face. "But what if it bites me!"

He groaned. "Frogs don't bite—they don't even have teeth."

So Lainie caught one—"HA!"—and added it to our haul.

Nineteen frogs.

Twenty-eight.

Thirty-seven.

Bobby and Tommy were wearing brand-new white sneakers. I watched as Bobby lost his balance, causing him to drag a foot in the muddy water.

"You're getting your sneakers dirty," I warned.

Bobby looked at me, puzzled, like I was speaking a foreign language.

"What's more important?" Tommy demanded. "Catching frogs or keeping your sneakers clean?"

"What do you think Mom's going to say?" I shot back.

Jimmy laughed. "Mom's not here, in case you didn't notice."

By now everybody had become obsessed with catching frogs. More and more of them got crammed into the bucket.

"Fifty!" Jimmy cried, staring into the mass of squirming green creatures. "That's a whole lotta frogs."

Johnny let out a triumphant whoop. "We're rich!"

Looking at Johnny made me cringe. He was a total wreck. Somehow he had managed to get a streak of mud on his forehead. Tommy and Jimmy were filthy too. Their shoes, jeans, and jerseys were mud spattered. I had managed to stay relatively clean.

"That's enough," Jimmy said, standing up straight. "Let's give it a rest."

"What's the final count?"

Jimmy smiled. "Sixty-three."

I did the math in my head: 63 frogs = 126 soggy eyes.

"A world record!" Johnny cried.

"Pretty close," Jimmy agreed. "C'mon, Ralphie, give me a hand."

He found a stick and inserted it through the bucket handle. With Jimmy carrying one end and me lifting the other, we managed to carry the heavy bucket back to our house.

Dad came outside, curious to see what all the commotion was about. When he peered into the bucket his eyes grew wide.

"Frogs!" Bobby yelled. "Look, Daddy, we got a million."

"Sixty-three." Jimmy smiled. "We hit the mother lode!"

Dad stood up. For a long moment he stared at my brothers, every one of them filthy and reeking of swamp mud. Then he leaned forward to take another look in the bucket.

"My God."

I didn't know how he would react, but I could

see that he was angry. I'm not sure if it was the *father* in him that was furious to see us sopping wet, new Keds sneakers soaked through on a cold day—maybe he worried we'd catch pneumonia—or if it was the *naturalist* in him who was outraged that his kids would endanger the lives of God's innocent creatures.

Or maybe a little bit of both.

"What do you think you're doing?" he demanded.

"We caught—" Lainie began, but he cut her off.

"I see what you caught," he barked. "You captured those frogs and took them away from their home."

Nobody said anything.

"Where did they live?"

"The swamp," Jimmy said, pointing.

"C'mon," Dad said firmly. "It's not too late to make this right."

He picked up the heavy bucket as if it weighed no more than a feather and carried it toward the woods. Dad walked with long, easy strides, and we had to hurry to keep up with him. When he reached the swamp, he unceremoniously dumped the frogs back into the water.

What a sight that was! An incredible green waterfall of amphibians! When they hit the muddy water the creatures paused for a few seconds, as if stunned by their good fortune. Then they roused themselves, one by one, and began darting off to every corner of the swamp.

After Dad left, I noticed Johnny had a sad expression on his face.

"I want my frog!"

"Dad's right," I said. "The swamp is their home—this is where they belong."

"Yeah," Lainie agreed. She touched Johnny's forehead where there was a slash of half-dried mud. "And right about now you belong in the bath!"

Me eating with the rest of the clan

The In-Betweener

Mom stood at the washing machine next to a laundry basket overflowing with wet, dirty clothes from our swampy frog-catching expedition.

"I've never seen such filthy clothes," she muttered. "Look at this."

She held up a pair of sneakers—Tommy's, I guessed—except they weren't new or white anymore. It looked like someone had dunked them in a pool of thick black mud. Which wasn't far from the truth.

"I bought these sneakers two weeks ago." She shook her head. "This swamp mud is like glue. . . ."

She dropped the sneakers—*thump thump*—into the washer. Then she dumped in the rest of the clothes.

"You'd think the kids would notice what was happening, wouldn't you?" Mom continued. "I mean, you'd think they'd be smart enough to see that they were surrounded by mud and maybe, just *possibly*, a little voice in their head would say, 'This isn't such a smart idea. We shouldn't be doing this.'"

"I know." I spoke in my smallest voice, maybe hoping she'd forget I was there, but she swiveled around to face me.

"You were there, too, weren't you?"

"Uh, well, sort of," I mumbled.

"Sort of?"

"Yeah, I was," I admitted.

She folded her arms. "So why didn't you do something?"

I didn't meet her gaze because I knew exactly what she meant. I was the oldest kid at the great

16

swamp fiasco, which meant that I was *in charge.*
I should have stopped it when the mud started
flying.

"I tried to," I said feebly.

Her expression turned skeptical. "Tried?"

"I told them to stop, but they didn't listen. . . ."
That sounded pretty lame, so I let my words
peter out.

Anyway, deep down, in that part of me that was
still a ten-year-old boy and not the Oldest Kid in
the Family, I knew it wasn't fair to blame it on my
brothers and sister. Mom hadn't been there, so she
didn't get it. And I couldn't find the right words to
tell her. How could I explain how excited we got
when the first pair of soggy eyes suddenly materialized, floating on the surface of the swamp? How
could I get her to understand what it felt like to
capture the first frog of spring, to hold that wild
squirming creature with its panicked heart in my
bare hands?

Mom stepped closer, a frustrated expression
on her face. She wasn't very tall, so we stood
eye-to-eye.

"What are we going to do about the kids?" she asked wearily.

It was a question she'd asked me a dozen times before. I hesitated, not sure what to say. For some reason, Mom never included me when she complained about "the kids." I guess it didn't occur to her that I was a kid too. And it never occurred to me, either.

That was my unusual role in the Fletcher family. Not one of the grown-ups, but not really one of the kids, either. I was sort of in between. Not yet a teen, more like a *tween*. At times it felt like a lonely place to be.

"I'm serious," she persisted. "What are we going to do about the kids?"

In my head I pictured Jimmy and Tommy and Bobby and Johnny and Joey—all their stunts and schemes and crazy antics. For the most part, Lainie acted in a civilized manner, but my brothers? That was a whole different story.

"I, uh, I don't know," I mumbled.

It wasn't a satisfying answer, but at that moment it was the best, most honest one I could come up with.

Jimmy and me

Marsh Field

I LIVED IN Marshfield, though we didn't pronounce it how you might expect. If you get a checkup, the doctor says, "Open your mouth and say ahhhh!" That *ahhhh* was the very sound we made when we spoke the name of our town: M*ahhhhhhhhh*shfield (that was the Massachusetts accent in the 1960s). I feel like I should apologize to the *r* in Marshfield because when we said that word we forgot it, or simply ignored it.

19

Marshfield means a *field of marshes*. My family lived inland, in a wooded area, but you didn't have to drive very far toward the ocean before you found yourself passing miles and miles of salt marshes. Though I often saw those marshes, I was curious about what it would feel like to be inside one of them.

One Saturday Dad's best friend, Dexter Harris, took us clamming. We would dig for them in a clam flat, but to get there we first had to pass through a marsh field. While we hiked, Dexter tried to educate us.

"A salt marsh is an important place in nature," he explained. "All kinds of birds, plants, insects, and fish live here. This place is teeming with life."

Lainie wrinkled her nose. "It smells stinky."

Dexter smiled. "That's the smell of the mud in low tide. You'll get used to it. So how are you guys doing? Tommy? Everything okay?"

Tommy chewed his lower lip. "No."

"What's wrong?" Jimmy asked.

"I don't like this place," Tommy muttered.

We reached a tiny stream. It was a small gap, barely a foot wide. We stepped over easily—everybody except Tommy.

"I can't!"

"C'mon," Dexter urged. "It's no big deal. Just step across."

"No!" Tommy objected. He looked down, eyes wild with fear and panic. "There's mud down there! There's quicksand!"

"There's no quicksand," Lainie assured him. Suddenly her eyes narrowed; she glanced up at Dexter. "Is there?"

"Probably not, though you do need to be careful," he told her. "If you're in the mud when the tide comes in, you could get stuck. I heard one guy got stuck in the mudflat when the tide came in, and the mud swallowed his car."

I blinked at him. "Really?"

He nodded. "But I seriously doubt there's any quicksand around here. C'mon, Tommy, all you've got to do is step over to the other side. It's not far at all. You can do it!"

"No!" Tommy cried.

Jimmy shook his head in disbelief. "What a baby!"

"Shhh," Dexter told him. "Making fun of him won't help. C'mon, Tommy, we gotta move. I promised your mother we'd bring home a bucket of steamers, and she's going to be mighty mad if we don't."

"I can't—" Tommy pleaded. So Dexter picked him up and swung him to the other side.

"Oh!" Tommy gasped, amazed to find himself on solid land instead of getting sucked down into the ooze.

We continued trekking through the marsh. My brother stayed miserable. The moment we reached the tiniest rivulet, the smallest gap, he halted and wouldn't budge. Each time Dexter had to lift him to the other side.

Gradually Tommy began to relax, which was a relief. Now I could stop worrying about him and start to appreciate my surroundings. The marsh was full of birds: gulls and terns and red-winged blackbirds. I loved the feel of the spongy ground and being enveloped by the tall, tall grass. The wind singing through the grass made a soft, high-pitched sound. Down low, beneath the tops of the grass, I felt cocooned and protected from the wind.

"The marsh is the place where the ocean shakes hands with the land," Dexter said.

I loved that thought and wanted to remember it always. I was a kid who loved the sound of words. I marveled at how they could paint a mind picture, how they could work together to create a mood or feeling. When I heard a word or a thought that caught my attention, I wrote it down in a little notebook I kept hidden between my box spring and mattress. I didn't know it then, but that little notebook would become precious to me. It would serve as a piggy bank of language, words, and ideas I would draw upon again and again as I became a writer.

Tommy and Jimmy

Pocketful of Trouble

MOM ALWAYS EMPTIED our pants pockets before she threw them in the washing machine. She could tell which pants belonged to which kid according to what she found tucked in those pockets.

My pockets usually contained a small notebook and my Bic pen.

In Jimmy's pockets Mom might find rocks, fossils, scraps of rope, carved wood, metal ball bearings, stuff like that.

Tommy's: marbles, money, plastic army guys.

Lainie's: shells, beach glass, colorful leaves.

Bobby: acorns, bottle caps, dandelion heads.

Johnny: action figures and Matchbox cars.

Emptying our pants pockets before washing them seemed like a sensible idea, but it could be hairy for Mom because she never knew what she might discover. Once when she reached into the pocket of a pair of jeans, she felt something warm and smooth—milkweed silk!

Another time she reached in and was shocked to feel something wriggling—a tiny toad. Jimmy had found it by the small creek that ran behind our house and stuck it in his pocket. With toad in hand, Mom marched downstairs and gave Jimmy a stern lecture about the mistreatment of animals. She and Dad often preached that "every life is sacred in God's eyes" and shouldn't be harmed. They were strict about that.

Jimmy felt bad—nobody loved nature any more than he did. He had carefully tucked the toad into his front pocket, intending to set it free later, but had forgotten to take it out. Luckily, the toad wasn't harmed. Mom directed Jimmy to release the creature in the woods, which is what he did.

Given all that commotion, nobody should have been surprised by what happened a few days later. Tommy found a piece of a wasp nest on the ground, brownish gray, about the size of a tennis ball. He showed it to me; we could see rows and rows of wasp larvae lined up inside the comb. They seemed to be dormant.

That weekend our family took a trip to Fall River, Massachusetts, to visit Grandma Maggie and Grandpa Fletcher. On Sunday when we got back home, Lainie got out of the car first and scampered to the back door. Peering through the glass, she saw something that gave her pause.

"What is it?" Jimmy demanded. "C'mon, open the door —I've got to pee!"

"There's a bunch of big flies buzzing around the kitchen," Lainie managed, standing on her tiptoes. "No, wait! It's not flies. I think they're bees!"

"Let me see," Jimmy said, pushing past her. "Hey, they're not bees; they're wasps!"

Staring through the glass, I could see them flying around—a fleet of wasps.

"Holy smokes," Dad softly exclaimed. "The house is infested!"

"So what do we do now?" Lainie put her hands on her hips.

"Where will we sleep?" Bobby asked.

"In the woods," Jimmy told him.

"But I don't want to sleep in the woods." Bobby glanced around uneasily. "It's spooky out there."

"We can stay at Terry and Dexter's house," Mom said. "They'll put us up for the night."

"I better call the exterminator," Dad muttered.

"Definitely." Mom nodded. "Call them first thing in the morning."

"I will," Dad promised.

Jimmy grinned and shook his head.

"What's so funny?" Mom demanded.

"You guys are always saying that every life is sacred in God's eyes," Jimmy reminded her. "But the exterminator? I mean, the exterminator's one and only job is to *kill* bugs."

Mom gave him a murderous look. "Be quiet. I'm not in the mood."

By doing some detective work, I was able to piece together what had happened. Tommy must have stuck the wasp nest in his pants pocket and forgotten about it. Before we went to Fall River, he left his dirty pants behind a chair in the corner of his bedroom, so Mom never found them. We were gone for the whole weekend. During that time, the warm air inside the house must have roused the wasplings from their slumber. They must have gotten hungry, hungry enough to crawl out of Tommy's pocket and start flying around in search of food. I told everyone my theory.

"Sorry," Tommy told Mom.

But she wasn't having any of that.

"Don't 'sorry' me, Tommy. Next time remember to put your dirty pants in the hamper so I can wash them."

"I will," he said meekly. "I promise."

For the next few days, Mom stayed mad at

Tommy. I guess we all did. Still, I felt a stab of stubborn admiration at Tommy's love of the raw outdoors, not to mention his fearlessness. How many kids would find a nest crammed with wasp larvae and stick it in his pants pocket?

Jimmy and me

Big Brother
Shadow

W HEN I WAS a kid, families tended to be bigger than they are today. My friend Freddy also lived on Acorn Street. He had nine siblings, including a bunch of older brothers. His brother Donny passed down sharp-looking sweaters to Freddy and taught him how to dance to songs by the Lettermen and the Four Seasons, plus how a dab of Brylcreem would keep his hair in place.

I didn't have a big brother to teach me important stuff like that. And I didn't have much privacy, either. There were ten people jammed into our small house, and we only had one bathroom. One! In the morning I had to wait my turn along with everyone else. Now that I was older, I desperately wanted time when I could be alone by myself, with no parents, brothers, or sisters to bother me.

One Saturday Mom planned a family outing to Benson Wild Animal Farm in New Hampshire. I always liked visiting Benson's when I was little—they let you pet and feed the animals—but I'd outgrown the experience years ago. Saturday morning my stomach felt queasy when I woke up, which gave me a faint glimmer of hope.

"I don't feel good," I mumbled at breakfast. (True.)

"Have a bowl of cereal," Mom advised.

"I did, but I still feel sick." (True, sort of.)

She studied me closely. "What's going on?"

"I feel like I'm going to throw up." (Not true.)

Throw up must have been the magic words,

because Dad immediately lowered the newspaper and stared at me.

"Did you say you feel like throwing up?"

"Uh-huh," I mumbled without looking at him.

Dad turned to look at Mom. "It's a long ride up to Benson's. The last thing we need is a kid vomiting in the car. Maybe he should say home."

She took another look at me. "He shouldn't be alone if he's sick."

"So what do you suggest?" Dad asked.

She shrugged. "I suppose I could stay home with him."

"I don't feel *that* sick," I quickly put in. "Hey, nobody has to stay home and take care of me, okay? I'll be fine."

Dad smiled. "I think he can take care of himself for one day."

I rolled my eyes. "I'm not three years old."

"All right." Mom nodded. "You can have soup with saltines for lunch. If you start feeling better, you can work on your Boy Scout stuff."

"Yeah," Jimmy chimed in. "Those knots of yours are NOT very good."

He grinned at his own cleverness. Anyway, he was right—my knot-tying skills were weak—so I let it pass.

For the next fifteen minutes I had to sit at the table, careful to continue looking miserable and at the same time hide the joy I could feel rampaging through me.

"I hope you feel better, Ralphie," Bobby murmured.

Jimmy flashed me a sour look. I knew he didn't want to go to Benson's, either. "If you're sick, then my name is Davy Crockett."

"I am sick," I insisted. "I—"

"Save it," he snapped.

I wasn't sure what I should do while I waited for them to get ready. Get dressed? No. I figured the wisest thing would be for me to climb back into bed, so that's what I did. After what seemed like forever, I finally heard everybody leave the house. Moments later, our car drove away.

I sprang out of bed and stared at myself in the mirror. I had achieved the impossible. HOME ALONE. I had the whole day to myself. I walked slowly through the rooms, one by one. Lainie had taped a big NO TRESPASSING sign to her bedroom door, but I barged in and lounged on her bed. Who could stop me? I did the same in Mom and Dad's room. Then I went to the bunk where Tommy slept. On a whim, I lifted his mattress and found several of my "lost" baseball cards hidden there. Why was I not surprised?

Pretty soon I had to use the bathroom. On this day I could take my sweet time, which is exactly what I did. For once in my life, I didn't feel rushed.

My stomach had made a miraculous recovery, so I went to the kitchen and helped myself to another bowl of cereal. Then I turned on the TV and stretched out on the couch. I couldn't find anything exciting to watch, but that wasn't the point. The TV was mine. It was a luxurious feeling to realize that I, and only I, could choose the channel, and nobody would argue with me.

After a while, I felt a little restless and decided to go outside. None of my friends were around, so I decided to take a stroll down Acorn Street. I felt free and easy. The summer sun warmed my neck and shoulders, casting a bright shadow in the shape of a person ahead of me. I had no particular place to go, so I followed a few steps behind that shadow.

The shadow pulled me along, and I was more than content to follow in its wake. When he turned left at Moraine Street, I turned left too. When he slowed down, I slowed down. We continued walking. He led me past the Tophams' house and continued toward town. I wondered where we were heading. Maybe we'd get an ice cream, or some penny candy at the general store. I didn't much care what we did. In the family, in school, in the Boy Scouts, I had always taken a leadership role, and that could be tiresome. For once in my life, it felt good to be a follower.

I pretended the shadow was my older brother, a kid with long legs who set a brisk pace. I had to scurry to keep up with him—zigging when he zigged, zagging when he zagged—and I couldn't have been happier going along for the ride.

Until he disappeared.

"No, wait!"

Thick clouds had swept in, blocking out the sun.

The spell was broken; the shadow had vanished. I stood there by the side of the road, unsure what I should do. After a while I just went home.

I opened a can of Campbell's soup and stood in the kitchen, waiting for the stove to warm up. My belly made that empty-stomach sound. But another part of me felt empty too. I felt as if I had lost someone important—the shadow of the big brother I never had.

What I did have was five brothers and two sisters who would soon be marching through that door. So I savored my freedom and devoured my soup (along with a whole stack of Ritz crackers) in front of the TV.

Me, Jimmy, Tommy, and Bobby

Boy Scouts

ANDY, STEVE, JIMMY, and I joined the Boy Scouts. We had to wear green uniforms with weird kerchiefs and funny-looking hats, but none of us minded because the Boy Scouts was tremendous fun. For one thing, scouting was chock-full of dangerous activities. Our scoutmaster taught us how to wield an axe, carve with a pocketknife, and light a match to start a campfire, things we'd never in a million years be allowed to do at home.

In the beginning we spent time learning how to tie various knots: half hitch, clove hitch, square knot, bowline, and a few others. This skill didn't come as easily to me as it did to Jimmy. My brother's hands seemed to have a special intelligence of their own, gracefully threading the rope under and over, making a square knot in a matter of seconds. Jimmy became known as the Knot King in our troop, and instructed all the younger kids in the proper way to tie knots.

I loved scouting. We got to hike, sleep in a tent, stay up as late as we wanted. We cooked our own food over a roaring fire. When we got home from a camping trip, happy and exhausted, all my clothes smelled like smoke.

One Friday afternoon Tommy watched Jimmy and me ready our backpacks for a two-night camping trip. I was ten; Tommy was seven.

"I want to go camping too," he said wistfully.

Mom smiled. "Someday you can join the Boy Scouts too."

"Can I?" Tommy begged. "Please, Mom?"

"Seems to me that scouting is a form of

supervised mayhem," Dad said, rubbing his chin thoughtfully. "Come to think of it, Tommy, it might be the perfect activity for a boy like you."

"I'm gonna make a bonfire when I'm in the Boy Scouts!" Tommy yelled.

"It's not just fooling around," Jimmy cautioned. "You gotta follow the rules."

True. There was a lot more to the Boy Scouts than fun and games. Scouting involved a way of being. It had a particular code of conduct; you were expected to follow certain rules. All Scouts had to memorize the Boy Scout oath: "On my honor, I will do my best to do my duty to God and my country and to obey the Scout Law; to help other people at all times; to keep myself physically strong, mentally awake, and morally straight."

Our scoutmaster, Mr. Briggs, wanted to grow our troop, so he encouraged us to bring our younger brothers to join. But I felt some trepidation about including Tommy. The Boy Scout oath was: *Be prepared.* How could you possibly be prepared for a wild child like Tommy?

♦ ♦ ♦

During camping trips Mr. Briggs had peculiar names for what we ate and drank. Kool-Aid was *bug juice*. Hot dogs were *tube steaks*. Some things we cooked were surprisingly delicious—Boy Scout stew, for example. When we returned from one camping trip, I mentioned this to Mom.

"Is that a fact?" She nodded, thinking. "Say, why don't you and Jimmy cook Boy Scout stew for supper tomorrow night?"

That was the LAST thing I'd expected her to say.

I exchanged a quick look with Jimmy. "Really?"

She shrugged. "Sure, why not?"

So that's what we did. I gave Mom a list of ingredients we needed: onions, carrots, hamburger meat. The next afternoon at five o'clock, the whole family gathered to watch Jimmy prepare a place for the fire in our backyard.

"Can I help?" Tommy pleaded.

Jimmy sighed. "I guess. Go get some firewood."

Minutes later, Tommy returned with a big armful.

"See?" He grinned. "I can be a real Boy Scout just like you guys!"

Jimmy lit the match and held it under a cluster of dry twigs.

"Don't make the fire too big," Dad cautioned.

Jimmy rolled his eyes. "Don't worry, Dad. We know what we're doing."

The flames flared into a crackling fire; fifteen minutes later there was a bed of hot coals. Jimmy carefully positioned three rocks to hold the pan off the fire. I cut up the onions and carrots and began frying them in the pan. When they were partially cooked, we added hamburger meat and a half cup of water, plus some salt, pepper, and garlic powder.

"Smells good!" Bobby exclaimed.

When the stew had finished cooking, I served it up. Tommy helped too. We ate it out of bowls, with slices of white bread to sop up the gravy.

"What do you think?" I asked Lainie.

"Not bad," she admitted.

Dad smacked his lips. "Very tasty!"

"Delicious," Mom agreed. "From now on, you guys cook supper, okay?"

I knew she was only kidding, but that comment made me feel good. Dad didn't cook a lick. "I couldn't boil water if my life depended on it," he freely admitted. I think this was the first time somebody other than Mom ever cooked a meal at our house. I felt proud that I knew how to do something my father couldn't do.

Jimmy and me

Daydreamer

Wₕₑₙ ɪ ᴡᴀꜱ in grade five an oceanographer visited our class. He brought in a right whale's baleen (the material that hangs down from the jaw of a whale and is used to filter small shrimp and plankton from the seawater). He passed it around so we could each have a turn holding it. This oceanographer talked nonstop about sharks, plankton, mollusks, and squid. He also explained how an oyster creates a pearl, which I found fascinating. It starts when a little piece of grit gets inside its shell. To protect itself, the oyster coats the grit with nacre or mother-of-pearl, a natural substance that's shiny. The oyster covers the grit with layer upon layer of nacre, which eventually creates the pearl.

"It's beautiful, no doubt," the oceanographer told us, holding up a pearl for everyone to see. "But never forget that it started with a piece of grit or sand. And that grit is still there, buried deep in the center of the pearl."

The oceanographer's visit excited our whole class. Afterward I dreamed about becoming an oceanographer. What a job that would be! I could explore the oceans like the great Jacques Cousteau, and protect them from harm.

I daydreamed constantly about my life and what my future might hold. Daydreaming felt like being in a trance—I was there, but I wasn't there. One afternoon, while riding home on the school bus, I was daydreaming when I felt someone poking my side.

"Ralph!" Andy prompted.

I blinked. "Huh?"

He shook his head. "Daydreaming again?"

"Yeah," I mumbled sheepishly.

It became one of my favorite pastimes. I daydreamed about playing baseball in the major leagues. I pictured myself racing back to spear a line drive, tumbling but miraculously hanging on to the ball and jumping up, my uniform streaked with dirt, while the astonished crowd roared its approval.

Other times I daydreamed about becoming a writer, creating wild adventures and baffling mysteries. I daydreamed about books, movies, war, and ghosts. In school, when I should have been paying attention to the teacher, I daydreamed about girls in our class.

Steve Fishman's house was surrounded by a large field filled with ragweed, Queen Anne's lace, thistle, and milkweed. In October, after the temperatures plunged, the milkweed pods started cracking open, releasing a stream of tiny silver balls. I thought they looked like little spaceships, flashing in the sun, floating all over the neighborhood. My daydreams were like that, spilling out of my head and drifting into the air.

I daydreamed about sleeping in a faraway wilderness, tucked in a cozy tent. Boy Scout camping trips had opened up that world to me. Usually these overnight trips involved only our troop, but once we went camping with another troop. Their scoutmaster was Mr. Schnayerson, a man with a passionate personality that made a sharp contrast to the mild, soft-spoken Arnold Briggs, our troop leader. Mr. Schnayerson gathered us at the beginning of the hike and gave a short, inspirational talk. He challenged us to "hone our vision" and to "summon the courage to follow our dreams."

During the hike some of the younger kids had trouble keeping up; Mr. Schnayerson asked me to accompany them while he and Mr. Briggs went ahead to locate our campsite. At one point Scotty Heimbecker, the youngest kid in Mr. Schnayerson's troop, tripped on a tree root and badly twisted his ankle. I had studied first aid, so I treated his foot the best I could. I didn't have any ice in my pack, though luckily I had brought an Ace bandage. I carefully wrapped Scotty's injured ankle, using a straight

stick to immobilize it and offer extra support. I told the boy to lean on me and not put any weight on his bad ankle. Together, we hobbled forward. Walking slowly, stopping often, we finally caught up to the others.

That night, while we were sitting by the campfire, Mr. Schnayerson motioned that he wanted to have a word with me. He led me a few steps from the fire.

"You handled that situation with Scotty really well," he said quietly. "I've noticed your leadership qualities."

"Really?" I was surprised to hear that.

"Not everybody can lead, but you can," he continued. "You know, Ralph, you could become a great man if you put your mind to it. I'm serious."

I shrugged with embarrassment, not sure what to say.

I never told anybody about that short conversation, until now. Who could I tell? And how could I tell it without sounding braggy? So it was one of those things I just kept to myself.

In the years that followed I didn't know how to categorize this experience—the words Mr. Schnayerson said to me that night, and their impact on me—though I daydreamed about it many times. *You could become a great man.* I wanted to believe him, but I wasn't sure. It felt like a small bit of sand stuck in the center of my soul. But it also gave me something to aspire to—the idea that I might have that potential buried deep inside my own pearl.

Bobby, Father McInnes, and Jimmy

Transistor Radio

W HEN I WAS young, transistor radios were like cell phones today—every kid wanted one. Andy Hunt saved up enough money to buy one of his own. Each night he'd climb into bed, insert the earplug, and listen to music as he drifted off to sleep.

"It's a beautiful thing," he told me, flashing a serene smile.

I envied him something fierce. I wanted a transistor radio of my own, badly. I ached for one. So I was especially thrilled when I opened a birthday present to find a jet-black pocket Zenith. The tiny radio was surprisingly powerful; it could pick up stations from as far away as Connecticut and New York.

That transistor radio became my secret shelter, a special place where I could go whenever I needed some privacy (which was every day). It was my connection to the outside world. The moment I switched on my radio and closed my eyes, a magical world of sound materialized. And, equally important, my chaotic family life disappeared for a little while.

I loved baseball. At night I had that little radio pressed to my ear as I listened to Curt Gowdy and Ned Martin broadcast Red Sox games on station WHDH. They described each game in such detail— the afternoon sunlight, the shadow creeping across the diamond—I felt like I was at the ballpark.

One night I stayed up way too late listening to the Red Sox battle the Yankees into extra innings. I had school the next day and knew I should turn off the radio, but the game was riveting and I couldn't switch it off. I just couldn't. The game moved to the bottom of the eleventh inning, with the Sox clinging to a one-run lead. One out. Two outs! I smelled victory. Then the Red Sox pitcher walked a batter, and the great Mickey Mantle came to the plate. Mantle was near the end of his career; still, he was very dangerous with a bat in his hand.

"Okay, here's the pitch . . ." Ned Martin said.

I heard it: *CRACK*.

"Uh-oh!" I could hear the alarm in Ned Martin's voice. "There's a LONG DRIVE TO CENTERFIELD. That ball is going . . . going . . . GONE! Home run! Yankees win. Mercy!"

I listened in disbelief as Yankee Stadium erupted in jubilation. Heartsick, I turned off the radio and closed my eyes, though I knew sleep wouldn't come easily that night.

◆ ◆ ◆

One of my favorite things was to lie in bed listening intently while the DJ counted down the top ten songs from the *Billboard* chart. He started by playing song #10. A few minutes later, he'd move to #9. The suspense kept building as he played the countdown. "Hard Day's Night" by the Beatles. "House of the Rising Sun" by the Animals. "Do Wah Diddy Diddy" by Manfred Mann.

"Only two songs left!" the DJ crowed. "Stay tuned to see what's this week's number one hit!"

Mom chose this inopportune moment to poke her head into my bedroom.

"It's late. You should turn off your radio."

"I will," I promised, though I couldn't turn it off just yet. The instant she left, I closed my eyes and sank back into the music.

The DJ announced, "This week the number two song is . . .'Baby Love' by the Supremes!"

My heart leapt. If "Baby Love" was #2 on the chart, by process of elimination, the #1 song had to be "Pretty Woman" by the great Roy Orbison.

And it was. I listened, enthralled by Orbison's amazing voice. I hung on every beat and note and word until the part where he sang, "Pretty woman, yeah yeah yeah . . ."

That was it—*there!*—my favorite part of my favorite song. At that moment it seemed as if the night melted and broke open like a chocolate cherry, dissolving in my mouth, flooding me with impossible sweetness and bliss. I felt positively holy, like I'd been blessed by the music, when I finally drifted off to sleep.

That little radio was a lifesaver to me. With my earphones plugged in and my thumb working the dial, I had a portal to another world that was all mine, secret and private.

Teen Princess

Square Dancing

Fɪꜰᴛʜ ɢʀᴀᴅᴇ: ɪ was eleven years old. We had all the usual activities for physical education (or PE, as we called it)—kickball, dodgeball, rope climbing, gymnastics—but one day the gym looked different. All the balls, mats, cones, and ropes had been put away. I was surprised to see that a record player had been set up on a small table flanked by two speakers. Our gym teacher, Shirley Trout, motioned us to gather around her.

"We're going to do something a little different today," Mrs. Trout declared. "Today we're going to be square dancing. I can promise you this—we'll have fun!"

Kids laughed, moaned, giggled, and gasped in disbelief. A few girls made little yelps of excitement. My friends and I looked around nervously. Square dancing? It was the LAST thing I expected from PE class.

"Get into groups of four," Mrs. Trout instructed us. "Each group should have two boys and two girls."

More giggles.

"It doesn't matter who you pick," she added. "By the end of class, every boy will have danced with every girl."

I tried to wrap my head around that.

"Do we have to?" a kid asked.

"Yes you have to." Mrs. Trout glared. "If you don't dance, you'll fail PE. I don't think you want an F on your report card, do you, Bruce?"

"No," he said meekly.

I joined a foursome along with Andy Hunt,

Janet Anderson, and Marilyn Swan. The girls smiled with anticipation as the first lively notes came out of the speaker—toe-tapping, fiddle-playing, knee-spanking bluegrass music. Mrs. Trout grabbed the microphone.

"We're gonna have ourselves a real hoedown in this here barn!" she drawled.

Andy rolled his eyes.

"Gentlemen, bow to your partner," Mrs. Trout cried.

Turning to Janet, I gave her a quick bow.

"Ladies!" Mrs. Trout called. "Curtsy to your partner!"

The girls curtsied gracefully, and the square dance began.

I'd never done this before, and so I found the whole thing monstrously confusing—the loud music, the rapid-fire instructions barked by Mrs. Trout, the sudden stops and starts and changes.

"Hold hands," Mrs. Trout called, "and circle to the left! Now circle to the right! Now swing your partner."

Another thing that rattled me: During the

square dance I had to continuously touch my partner. There was absolutely no way around it. It was only touching her hand, or her side, but still. It was a *girl's* hand. A *girl's* side. We had to stand so close to each other we were practically breathing the same air.

Swinging Janet Anderson (who was taller than me) made me feel dizzy, though I tried not to show it. I had just begun to get used to having Janet Anderson as my partner when the first round ended. The couples got scrambled, and I found myself with a new partner, Meg Dubois.

"Promenade your new partner," Mrs. Trout called. "Okay, now shake hands with your new partner!"

The music paused, and I tried to catch my breath. Around me other kids were laughing, giggling, and whispering. The girls seemed to revel in this new activity. A few of the boys liked it too, though this group did not include me. I felt awkward.

The music started up again. The square dance had multiple rounds. Two rounds later I found myself partnered with Lee Clapp. She was wearing a red dress, and it hit me she must have specially chosen to wear it because of the dance. Earlier in the day, I had noticed several girls in our class wearing fancy dresses. Some had even fixed up their hair. Now I knew why. Somehow the girls had found out about the square dance ahead of time. As usual, the boys didn't have a clue.

Lee's face was flushed. "Having fun?"

"Not really," I admitted. "Anyway, you look nice."

Shyly, she smiled. "Thanks."

Later, Mrs. Trout put another record on the stereo.

"Watch me," she instructed. "Follow my movements."

When the music started, Mrs. Trout began dancing and singing at the same time.

"Heel, toe, heel, toe, step baby step—OH! Heel, toe, heel, toe, step baby step. . . ."

I felt like an idiot moving my feet in that way. In desperation I glanced at the clock and was shocked to see that only twenty minutes had gone by. There were still another twenty minutes—an eternity!—until the class would end.

✦ ✦ ✦

After school I took a walk in the woods with Andy. He had been one of the few boys who enjoyed dancing.

I looked at him in disbelief. "You actually liked that?"

"Yeah, I thought it was a fun thing to do in gym," he told me. "You gotta admit it was a heckuva lot better than tumbling."

I said nothing.

"Why?" he asked. "You didn't like it?"

"No." I shook my head. "I didn't like having . . . a partner. You know, being paired up with a cute girl like Beth Byers or Lisa Kennedy."

Andy smiled. "Dancing with Beth Byers? You like that girl, don't you?"

"I don't know," I mumbled. "If I ever have a girl-friend, I want to choose my own girl."

At these words, Andy suddenly slammed on the brakes and stared at me in disbelief.

"They were your partners in a square dance!" He laughed. "You danced with each girl for maybe three minutes. Jeez Louise, Ralph, you make it sound like you were getting married to them!"

He was right, of course, but I couldn't help how I felt. I don't know exactly what I had found so unnerving about the square dance. I think it had something to do with being face-to-face with the girls. Their frank, bold smiles. The girls scared me, although the more I thought about them, they intrigued me too. They seemed to possess some secret knowledge I hadn't yet discovered. More fuel for my daydreams.

Jimmy and me

Gwen Givvens

ONE GOOD THING about Sunday school: It only lasted an hour. That and Gwen Givvens, the girl who sat directly behind me. She didn't go to my regular school, so Sundays were the only time I got to see her. Gwen hardly ever spoke. She was small, so much so it was hard to believe she was a fifth grader too. Mrs. Wrenham, our Sunday school teacher, encouraged us to bring in treats from home, but on the first Sunday I forgot. I had to sit there, trying to act like I didn't care while other kids tore into their goodies. Tantalizing smells of brownies, cookies, and Rice Krispies treats erupted around me. My stomach started rumbling.

"You like Necco Wafers?"

I was startled to realize Gwen Givvens had spoken to me.

"Well, yeah." I mean, who doesn't like Necco Wafers?

She offered me the roll. After a moment's hesitation, I reached out and removed one wafer—pink.

"Take a couple," she urged.

So I took two more Necco Wafers—yellow and gray.

Gwen gave me a sly smile. "Aha, lemon and licorice. Excellent choices."

The following week Mom packed me three Toll House chocolate-chip cookies for Sunday school. I had just taken my first chewy bite when a voice behind me whispered, "Want a Necco Wafer?"

"Thanks," I told Gwen. "But I've got a snack."

"This isn't just an ordinary snack, Ralph." She

screwed up her face and made her eyes sparkle. "These are *Necco Wafers.*"

I smiled. "Very true."

"Take a couple," she urged, offering me the roll. "They're small—like me."

"You're not *that* small."

"Thank God," she muttered, making a comical face.

It became our weekly ritual—talking about Necco Wafers. One Sunday when she offered me her roll of Neccos I removed the brown one: chocolate.

Gwen smiled. "The browns are my favorite."

My eyes grew wide. "Mine too!"

She nodded. "They're so good! So why do they only put a couple in every roll? You know what they should do? They should make a whole roll of just brown wafers. Wouldn't that be great?"

I looked at her closely, surprised to hear so many words spilling out of her. And she wasn't done yet.

"Do you know what Necco stands for?" she asked.

"Uh, no."

"New England Confectionery Company. Guess how I found out? My uncle works there."

"Wow. Does he get all the Neccos he wants for free?"

"No. But I think he gets a discount." She leaned toward me. "Wouldn't it be cool if he got paid in Necco Wafers?"

I nodded. "Yeah!"

✦ ✦ ✦

Soon the holidays arrived, Thanksgiving followed by Christmas. We had a Christmas party in Sunday school. Gwen wore a red dress.

"You look nice," I told her.

Blushing, she smiled. "Thanks."

They didn't have Sunday school over the Christmas vacation, so I didn't see her for a while. After New Year's Gwen wasn't in Sunday school that first week, or the next week, either. I missed seeing her.

"Do you know where Gwen is?" I asked our teacher.

"She's been sick," Mrs. Wrenham told me.

What's wrong with her? I wanted to ask, but I didn't. The flu had been going around.

The following week my family went to dinner at the Cracker Barrel restaurant. We hardly ever went out to dinner, so this was a BIG DEAL. We left the restaurant through the gift shop.

"No souvenirs," Mom warned.

"But, Mom . . ." Tommy whined.

She firmly shook her head. I was walking past the checkout counter, where I happened to see a basket. Leaning closer, I saw that it contained rolls of Necco Wafers. But these looked different. The sign said CHOCOLATE NECCO WAFERS.

I was stunned. A whole roll of nothing-but-chocolate Neccos! Luckily, I had enough pocket change with me to buy two rolls. I couldn't wait to show them to Gwen when she got back.

Swimming in the summer

Funsies and
Keepsies

NOWADAYS KIDS COLLECT things like Pokémon
cards or friendship bracelets. When I was a kid we
collected marbles. The smallest marble was a pee-
wee, followed by a cat's-eye, then a bogey, a mumbo,
and then a jumbo. The bigger the marble, the more
valuable it was. If a marble was a *crystal* (totally
clear inside), it had an even higher value.

I adored my marbles and spent countless hours
holding them up to the light, turning them this way

and that, peering into their interiors to see what might be inside. Like icicles, marbles seemed to sparkle with their own concentrated light. I loved the liquid way they poured out of my bag, and the peculiar *click-click-click* sound they made bumping against each other, as if those orbs might be speaking their own language. Gazing down at my marbles, I imagined I had my own personal solar system, a collection of tiny planets on my bedspread.

Marbles were like money, only better. If you had lots of marbles kids treated you like you were rich. And you *were* rich. Nobody doubted it.

If you collected marbles you had to have something to hold them in. I used a cloth bag that I'd made myself with a lot of help from my mother. She provided me with a needle, thread, and a piece of fabric.

"I recommend you double-stitch it to make it extra strong," Mom advised. "You don't want that seam to rip open."

So that's what I did. When I finished sewing the seam, I turned the bag inside out to hide the stitching. It worked great. Now I had a pouch to keep my treasures snug and secure.

My friends and I played a number of common marble games:

Ringer: Played in a large ring with thirteen marbles arranged in a cross in the center. The object was to use your marble as a "shooter" to knock the other marbles out of the ring.

Poison: The target is a shallow hole about six inches across and a half inch deep. Players shoot from behind a line three to five feet away. Each player tries to be the first to get his shooter into the hole. If successful, the shooter becomes "poison." After that, you can collect any marble that ends up within a hand span of the hole.

Boss-Out: First player shoots one marble. Second player tries to hit the first player's marble. If he does, that player collects both marbles.

Off-the-Wall: Players take turns rolling their marbles toward a curb or wall. Whoever has the closest marble to the wall collects all the other marbles.

We also made up games of our own: Knuckle-Down, Holies, Bogeys, Closeys, and Shooties.

You could buy marbles at the Woolworth's five and ten-cent store, not far from my house. They didn't cost much, but kids who simply bought their marbles didn't get much respect from other kids. Nope, you had to win them. You played against other kids, head-to-head. If you beat your opponent, you won the marble he played. We all knew famous stories about skilled players who amassed a fortune in this way. One time my good friend Freddy Fletcher (one of the other Fletchers—no relation—who lived down the street) went to school with only one marble. He risked playing it and won, and won again, and kept winning until that afternoon he triumphantly climbed onto the bus, his bag jammed with marbles.

It was exciting to win, but hard to lose, and harder still to watch one of my brothers get beat. One time Tommy took eight brand-new bogeys to school. He was eager to win more; unfortunately, he wasn't a very good player. An older boy challenged him to play Off-the-Wall. I watched Tommy lose his bogeys one after another, and I felt terrible. I could see what was happening and tried to get him to quit. His expression turned hard and desperate, but he shook me off, and soon all his marbles were gone.

Jim Dean, a kid from a nearby neighborhood, had one amazing crystal bogey, gorgeous aquamarine. One night I had a magical dream about that marble. I badly wanted Jim's crystal bogey, but he wasn't stupid. He knew what he had, and wasn't going to let it go for cheap.

"I'll play three of my bogeys against your crystal bogey," I offered.

Jim smirked in amusement, then shook his head. "No way."

"How many, then?"

"Six."

"Six!" I stared at him in disbelief. "You're nuts! Nobody's gonna play you six against one."

Jim shrugged. "Then I won't play."

"How about five?" I countered. "I'll play you five against your one."

He nodded. "Okay."

Game on. A half dozen kids followed us to a corner of the playground where a large circle had been marked out in the dirt. There was a hole, about five inches across, dug in the middle. The objective of the game was to be the first to shoot your marble into the "pot" (hole). You won if you got your marble in first—unless your opponent could get his marble into the pot on the very next shot. When that happened, the game would be declared a tie, and you started over.

There were different ways to shoot a marble. My buddies and I prepared to shoot by putting one hand on the ground directly behind the marble. When it was your turn, you propelled the marble forward, using the part of your forefinger between the first and second knuckles.

Jim had a reputation as one of the best players around, but I wasn't too bad myself. On my second shot, I tossed a bogey that landed two feet from the hole and scampered in.

Kids whistled. It was an amazing, improbable shot, and it set me up to win unless Jim could match my shot. All of a sudden, he looked concerned. His prized bogey was in peril.

"I call funsies!" he cried.

I couldn't believe my ears. When kids played marbles for *funsies*, it was understood that they were just playing for fun—nobody could lose or win any marbles. Playing for funsies allowed you to practice without pressure. But that had to be agreed on before the game started. Otherwise it was *keepsies*—you were playing for keeps, for real. Losing the game meant losing your marble.

"What?!" I sputtered. "This is keepsies!"

He folded his arms. "You didn't call it. And I called funsies."

"It's keepsies!" I insisted. "Why the heck do you think everybody's here watching?"

"I called funsies," Jim said for the third time.

"You've got to call it ahead of time!" I objected.

"I called it now, before you did." He went to stand beside the crystal bogey. "You still want to play?"

"What's the point?" I shouted. "No!"

I could feel my neck muscles straining, and tried to swallow down my rage.

"Okay, then," Jim said. He grabbed that crystal bogey and left.

I was furious, but I wasn't surprised. Arguments—even fistfights—involving marbles were common. Marbles was only a game, but a game with particular rules and rituals that took on tremendous importance for us all. Marbles mattered.

Andy tried to console me. "Let it go. Who needs that crystal bogey anyway?"

I do, I thought as we walked. I tried to shake off my fury, but I knew I'd have a bad taste in my mouth for a long time. What was the sense of having rules if you didn't follow them?

Ale's Woods

Mushrooms

Mushrooms grew everywhere in our neighborhood: in damp areas of the field or forest, under
shady trees, near swamps and streams. They
reminded me of small, helmeted soldiers, a secret
army that patrolled and controlled the forest. And
I loved their fantastic names: devil's snuffbox,
witch's cap, boletes, wine caps, chanterelles, giant
puffballs, jack-o'-lanterns . . .

"There are some wild mushrooms you can eat,"

Lainie declared at supper one night. "My teacher told us in school."

"That may be," Mom quickly interjected, "but mushrooms can be poisonous too. So whatever you do, don't eat any of them." She gave the little kids a pointed look. "Are you listening? Do you hear what I'm saying? Leave mushrooms alone."

A bunch of little heads bobbed up and down. "Okay, Mommy."

I had figured out that people were like mushrooms, in a way. Most were fine, or at least harmless, but a few could be dangerous. Take Barry O'Neil, a boy who moved into the neighborhood one summer. He didn't actually move in; he was a cousin to Ricky O'Neil, a kid who lived on a nearby street. At first Barry's easy smile gave me the impression that he must be a nice kid. But Barry turned out to be pure poison.

Although I noticed Barry a few times walking with Ricky down Acorn Street, the first time he caught my attention was at the beach. I spotted him standing near the top of the stairs that led from the parking lot down to the water. Other kids had gathered there too, including one kid who had a bag of marbles poised precariously at the top of the stairs.

I saw the whole thing clearly, as if it was happening in slow motion: Barry sidled over and slyly nudged that bag so that it toppled over. Marbles by the dozens began to pour down the stairs. Bogeys! Crystals! Clayeys! Countless tiny orbs flashed and sparkled and streamed like water. Ricky's friends frantically tried to help the boy corral his marbles once they landed, but other kids started grabbing them.

"Hey, those are mine!"

All the while Barry stood at the top, arms crossed, grinning broadly at the uproar he had created. And Ricky never suspected him.

That left a big impression on me. Stealing a bite of someone's doughnut was one thing, but messing with someone's marbles? That was cruel.

A few days later Andy, Steve, Freddy, and I met at the edge of the big field at the Fishmans' house. We wanted to plan a football game. My brother Bobby had come along too. He and Steve's youngest brother, Paul, were playing in the dirt about fifteen feet away. Glancing up, I saw Barry O'Neil and his cousin Ricky walking down the driveway toward us. When Barry reached Bobby he stopped and crouched down, I guess to talk to him.

"Let's make this a really big game," Freddy was saying. "We should invite over some kids from school."

I nodded. At the edge of my peripheral vision, I half noticed that Barry had picked up a dandelion stem topped by a globe of silver spores. Squatting, he showed it to Bobby.

"Isn't that cool?" Barry cooed in an inviting voice. "Open your mouth."

I froze. In that interval my brother obediently opened his mouth wide. When he did, Barry blew the spores into his mouth.

Bobby screamed.

"Hey!" I cried, running over. "What do you think you're doing!?"

Barry laughed; he and Ricky quickly sprinted away. Paul led Bobby into the house so he could get some water to rinse out his mouth.

"Somebody ought to punch that kid," I declared, watching Barry disappear into the distance.

Freddy smiled. "Where do I sign up?"

♦ ♦ ♦

Two days later Andy and I were in the Woolworth's store when we happened to run into Barry. I stalked over to him.

"Hey, sorry about your brother," he said, raising his hands. "I didn't mean nothing—I was just messing around."

"Next time you better mess with someone else," I warned.

"Okay, okay." He flashed his trademark easy smile.

I watched him wander over to a display of balsa wood airplanes. A moment later he drifted to the checkout counter. When the woman at the cash register turned away, Barry quickly snatched a box of Jujubes and ducked out of the store. Andy and I followed.

"We saw that," I told Barry.

"Bully for you." He offered the opened box. "Have some."

Andy shrugged and took a few, but I hesitated.

"What's wrong?" Barry asked.

"Ralph's a Boy Scout AND an altar boy," explained Andy. "He's practically a saint. No way he's going to eat stolen candy."

I didn't appreciate Andy teasing me like that in front of a kid we both didn't like, but I didn't know what to say, so I bit my tongue.

"C'mon," Barry persisted, waggling the box in my direction. "Live a little!"

Barry brought the box closer, so close the sweet smell of the Jujubes wafted up to my quivering nostrils.

"I can't take 'em back now," he pointed out. "They're already opened."

Which was true. So I grabbed the box and spilled some into my right hand: one yellow, one orange, one green, one cherry, and one purple; the Jujubes were the size of the eraser on a new pencil. I popped the green bead into my mouth first. After I polished it off, I ate the others, one by one by one.

I would have predicted that those Jujubes would have tasted nasty, or spoiled, or tainted in some way. But they were delicious. I felt guilt and amazement in equal parts. It didn't make sense. Barry was a total jerk, so how come my taste buds were popping wheelies in my mouth? I was a rule follower, for sure, so it was a secret thrill to enjoy the spoils of this minor theft.

With my relatives at a family reunion

Cousins by
the Dozens

My PARENTS EACH had seven siblings, and most of
them grew up to have giant families of their own.
I had cousins coming out of my ears, so many that I
had trouble remembering their names. Clumps of
cousins showed up at family reunions. They'd climb
out of their cars and blink in the sunlight with their
freckles and cowlicks and pale Irish skin. It felt
strange but also kind of cool to realize that we all
shared the same bloodline.

My cousins often came over for a visit: MarkPeterMaryBethPaulMichaelChristopher BillyGregJudy. I'd introduce them to my friends Andy and Steve, who couldn't believe their eyes.

Andy sputtered, "I've got eight cousins—you've got eight million!"

I smiled. "Not quite."

"Seriously, how many do you have?" he demanded.

"I, well, I really don't know," I admitted.

I went to my mother to get a solid number. "Mom, how many cousins do I have?"

"Lots."

"*Exactly* how many?" I persisted.

"Well, I don't know but we can easily figure it out," she said, grabbing a pencil. "Let's count up all the grandchildren. We'll start with the Collins side of the family."

> Jimmy and Winnie Collins: 2
> Norma and Cecil Clark: 7
> Mary Collins: 0
> Ruth and Paul McCullough: 7

Billy and Mary Collins: 5
Johnny and Jane Collins: 3
Eddie and Joan Collins: 5

Next she tallied up the grandchildren on the Fletcher side.

Paul and Louise Fletcher: 7
Ann and Bill Whalen: 5
Joan and Warren Charette: 6
Billy and Jeanette Fletcher: 4
Bernard and Nicole Fletcher: 5
John and Mary Beth Fletcher: 0
Margaret Fletcher and Bob Grant: 1

She took a few moments to add them up.

"Twenty-nine Collins cousins and twenty-eight Fletcher cousins. So you've got fifty-seven first cousins, if my math is right." She smiled at me. "But don't forget that you guys are cousins to them. If you throw in our eight kids, that makes a grand total of sixty-five cousins."

I let out a low whistle. "Wow."

✦ ✦ ✦

One day at a family reunion, I found myself playing catch with one kid who looked familiar in a Fletcherish kind of way. I wanted to find out for sure if we were first cousins, though I wasn't sure how to bring it up. Finally I just blurted the question.

"Are we cousins?"

He frowned. "Of course! I'm Billy Whalen."

"Oh, right." In my head I quickly scrambled up the Fletcher family tree. My father's sister Ann was married to Bill Whalen. In fact, they were my godparents. So this kid was most definitely my first cousin.

Most times I could sense when one of my cousins was around. A little voice in my head whispered, "Cousin close by!" But that voice didn't work 100 percent of the time. A few times I got fooled.

Our family had made plans to join a big gathering of the Fletcher tribe in Rhode Island. Grandma Maggie and Grandpa Fletcher would be there, plus all my uncles and aunts and cousins galore. Many of my cousins lived nearby, and I learned that some would bring along their own friends—kids who were not part of the family. The reunion took place on a beautiful July day. Someone organized a game of softball. Afterward the kids split up into two teams to play Capture the Flag. At one point I noticed a girl looking at me, half smiling. I'd never seen her before, and figured she must be one of my cousins' friends.

Toward the end of the game I found myself alone in the woods, or so I thought. The sound of crunching leaves made me whirl around. And there she was: the girl I'd seen earlier. She walked toward me, not the slightest bit shy.

"Hi."

I swallowed. "Hi."

I looked at her closely. She was kind of beautiful, with dark hair and olive skin, and a sleepy smile that warmed me from the inside out.

"What . . . what are you doing here?" I asked.

"Looking for you." Reaching out, she touched both my shoulders and gently squeezed. "Want to kiss me?"

Just like that: *Want to kiss me?*

I did want to kiss her. I took a half step closer,

and closer still. Now I could feel her breath, warm and sweet. I leaned forward until our bottom lips touched very lightly, but something made me pull back.

"You're . . ." I began.

She cocked her head. "What?"

"You're, we're, wait, you're not . . . ?" I stammered.

She smiled. "What?"

"You're not . . . related to me, are you?" I asked.

She giggled softly. "Yes, I'm related to you!"

She told me who she was; the familiar last name made my blood run cold.

"Then we can't," I said.

"Sure we can," she countered. She tried to kiss me again, but I spun out of her grip.

"But, we're cousins!"

"So what?" She grinned. "That's why God gave us cousins . . . to learn how to kiss."

"No it's not!" I figured she was kidding.

I started backing away from her. "I, uh, I better get back to the game."

She shrugged. "Okay, Ralph. It's your funeral."

Whatever that meant.

"This never happened," I hastened to. add.

She smiled. "But don't you kind've wish it did?"

"No!" I said, louder than I intended.

I sprinted back to the Capture the Flag game while her words kept jumbling around in my head. *But don't you kind've wish it did?* Maybe she was right—but no, she couldn't be right. After all, she was my first cousin. Still . . . I'd felt a thrill like I'd never before experienced in that moment . . . even if it ended before anything really happened.

Jimmy on a Boy Scout camping trip

Sky Hook and a
Bacon-Stretcher

I SAT AT the kitchen table watching Tommy try to memorize the Boy Scout law. Dad sat across from me, drinking coffee and reading the *Boston Globe.*

"Trustworthy, loyal, helpful, friendly, courteous, kind," Tommy began. Then he stopped and looked up helplessly. "I'm stuck, Ralphie. What's the next one?"

"Obedient." I couldn't resist adding, "No wonder you couldn't remember that one."

His eyes narrowed. "Why?"

"Because you never obey anyone," I shot back.

"Yes I do!" Tommy's eyes flared, but then his expression turned sly. "Anyway, I'm going to be a Boy Scout, just like you and Jimmy. Dad already bought me the uniform, right, Dad?"

Dad nodded.

"Being a Boy Scout is more than just wearing the uniform," I reminded Tommy. "A lot more."

My father was reading the newspaper. I didn't think he'd been listening to this conversation, but he now caught my eye and motioned me to follow him. We went through the back door and onto the porch.

"What did I do?"

"You were a little hard on Tommy."

"Yeah, but he—"

"Deserves to have a clean slate," Dad said, yanking my sentence in a different direction than I had intended. "He shouldn't feel like he's trouble before he's even gone to his first Boy Scout meeting."

"I guess," I said reluctantly.

"Anyway, I'm trying to look on the bright side. Maybe Boy Scouts will be good for him."

"But he's my brother," I pointed out. "If he starts acting up, I'll get blamed too."

Dad shook his head. "You take care of yourself. You're not responsible for what your brother does."

That was the first time I'd heard that one. I was supposed to be Mr. Responsibility, a role that had two parts. I had a responsibility to set a good example, sure, but I also felt responsible for how my siblings acted.

"Just give him a chance," Dad concluded. "I seriously believe Tommy's ready for the Boy Scouts."

Maybe, I thought. *But are the Boy Scouts ready for him?*

Ready or not, Troop 88 accepted Tommy as one of its members. Mom sewed two cloth 8 patches onto the shoulder of his uniform, just as she had for Jimmy and me. Mr. Briggs asked if I wanted him to be in my patrol, which would put him under my leadership.

"If you don't mind, I'd rather not have him," I said.

Mr. Briggs smiled. "I understand."

Tommy got assigned to Andy Hunt's patrol. He had waited a long time, and he was thrilled to be in the Scouts—finally!

✦ ✦ ✦

On Tommy's first camping trip things got off to a rocky start, though it wasn't all his fault. We set up our camp not far from another troop. Mike Simon, our assistant scoutmaster, immediately sent Tommy on a mission to the other troop to borrow a few things, necessary items Mr. Simon had forgotten. Tommy hurried off, eager to help. After a half hour I noticed he hadn't returned, so I went to check in on him. He looked tired when I found him.

"What are you doing?" I asked.

"Mr. Simon said I have to get some stuff from the other troop," he explained.

"What kind of stuff?"

"A sky hook and a bacon-stretcher," Tommy explained. "Mr. Simon said we'll need that in the morning, especially the bacon-stretcher. He said if you don't use one, the bacon will get all scrunched up. They keep sending me to talk to different patrol leaders, but nobody has one. I have to ask one more guy."

I understood. There was a tradition of playing tricks on brand-new Boy Scouts. It was harmless in a way, but still . . .

"Are you really that gullible?" I asked. "There's no such thing as a bacon-stretcher! Or a sky hook!"

He looked flabbergasted. "There's not?"

"No!" I shook my head. "Have you ever seen Mom use a bacon-stretcher when she cooks bacon? Do you really think there's a hook that hangs from the sky? What would it hang from?"

"No, but . . ." Tommy looked confused. "So those guys were all lying?"

"They were playing a practical joke on you," I explained. "They did the same thing to me when I first joined the Scouts. C'mon, let's go back."

Early next morning we took a short hike to a small lake. We returned to the campground just as a light rain began to fall. Mr. Briggs gathered our whole troop inside a lean-to where we could eat lunch. He brought the patrol leaders outside to plan the rest of the afternoon.

That's when it happened.

"WE'RE UNDER ATTACK!" someone cried.

"What's going on?" Mr. Briggs demanded.

"Rocks!" one boy exclaimed.

"Yeah, someone's throwing rocks at the lean-to!" another boy yelled breathlessly. "Big ones!"

Scouts began pouring out of the lean-to. I was shocked to see that several kids had army knives in their hands.

"STOP RIGHT THERE!" Mr. Briggs yelled.

The troop froze.

"What do you think you're doing?" Mr. Briggs demanded.

"We're going to find whoever's throwing rocks—"

"Not like that you're not!" Mr. Briggs snapped. "Running around with army knives is a great way to hurt someone. Turn around and put that stuff away. That's an order!"

The kids slunk back inside. Common suspicion

led Jimmy, Andy, and me to go check on Tommy. We found him in the lean-to sprawled out on an old mattress with other kids his age.

"What's all the fuss?" he calmly asked.

"Somebody threw some rocks at the lean-to," I told him. "Nothing to worry about."

Things settled down. Mr. Briggs asked the patrol leaders to organize a map-reading activity. He passed around maps and handed out compasses.

BOOM! Rumble, tumble, BOOM! Ba-da BOOM!

"What the—" Steve Fishman sputtered.

"WE'RE UNDER ATTACK!" kids yelled for the second time.

"THEY'RE ATTACKING US AGAIN!"

"SOMEONE'S WHIPPING ROCKS AT OUR LEAN-TO!"

I marched over to Tommy.

"What were you doing just now?" I asked.

"Nothing."

"Nothing?" I asked skeptically. "Where were you when the rocks hit?"

"Lying on this mattress," he told me. "But I think maybe I saw the kids who threw the rocks!"

"Yeah? What did they look like?"

"I don't know. They looked older. Maybe high school kids."

He looked at me, all wide-eyed and innocent, but I still wasn't convinced. I wondered if Tommy could possibly have stepped outside, lobbed some large rocks onto the lean-to without being noticed, and then ducked back inside a split second before they struck the roof.

Could he? Yes.

Would he? Oh, yes.

Jimmy approached me. "Where was Tommy when the rocks hit?"

"He says he was lying on the mattress," I replied.

Jimmy flashed a knowing smile. "Yeah, *lying* all right."

We glanced over at Tommy. By the peaceful way he was sitting, you would have thought he was the Buddha or Jesus Christ. I remembered Dad's words: *Just give him a chance.* I wanted to, but I got nervous when Tommy suddenly started acting like an angel. Could I prove that my brother was involved in the rock-throwing incident? No. But I had learned a long time ago that you could never put anything past Tommy—ever. I made a mental note to keep close tabs on him during the rest of the campout.

Jimmy, Lainie, and me

The Marshfield Fair

MARSHFIELD HELD A big Lobster Festival every summer, but it was the Marshfield Fair that put our town on the map. This huge, sprawling, old-fashioned, over-the-top country fair featured giant pumpkin contests, pie bake-offs, 4H booths with blue-ribbon pigs, carnival games, the whole she-bang. The Marshfield Fair drew people from all over the South Shore, and even as far as Boston.

In mid-July the sight of huge tents being erected

on the Marshfield fairgrounds got my blood pumping. I immediately started pestering my parents for extra jobs I could do, anything to earn money for the fair.

Finally the big day arrived. Mom dropped off Jimmy and me at ten in the morning.

"You've got three dollars so spend wisely," she said. "You need to make it last all day. I'll pick you guys up right here at four o'clock."

Back then it was common to be left at the fair all day without an adult.

"But we want to stay for the fireworks!" I told her. "Andy says we can get a ride home with him."

"Yeah, please, Mom?" Jimmy begged.

"Oh, all right." Sighing, she reached into her purse and gave us each another dollar. "You'll need to buy something for supper."

I leaned over and gave her a quick kiss.

"You're the best, Mom!"

"You bet I am."

Jimmy found his friend Ricky Topham waiting for him inside the main gate. I quickly located my friends: Andy, Steve, Freddy, and Jim Dean. The five of us made a beeline for the mouthwatering food stalls: fried dough, corn dogs, French fries, and not one but two cotton candy machines. People were already lined up to buy it. I watched, mesmerized, as the woman skillfully twirled a white paper cone, gathering the silken blue/white/pink strands.

"Looks like a little cloud of sugar," I remarked.

Steve glanced at me quizzically. "Why don't you write a poem about it?"

"Maybe I will," I told him.

"You should try to get the merit badge for writing poetry," Jim Dean suggested. Then he made a big show of slapping his forehead. "Oh, I forgot, they DON'T HAVE A MERIT BADGE FOR POETRY!"

True: The Boy Scouts had a merit badge for pottery, even basket weaving, but not poetry. I guess the Boy Scout powers-that-be didn't think poetry "merited" its own badge. The journalism badge was the closest you could get, but that one had nothing to do with poetry.

"I can't hear you," I said, eyes closed, letting the fresh strands of cotton candy dissolve in my mouth.

Nobody wants to be teased, so in general I found it wise to hide my interest in writing from my friends. But the Marshfield Fair truly was a feast for a young writer, offering all kinds of inspiration. Like when I went on the Ferris wheel, it felt like there was a little wheel of fear, a whirring gyroscope of terror, spinning in my stomach. The first thing I did when I got home that night was to go up to my bedroom, take out my notebook, and write down that sentence. It felt like a seed for a story or a poem I could write later.

Ants

As I watched the ants queen,
I found she is very mean,
And not a very good ruler.
She has to command,
The ants to take the sand
Out of the hole,
And onto the land.

Ralph Fletcher

Poetry

I n the fall I was pleased when Mrs. Larsen devoted two whole weeks to writing poetry. That had never happened before. The first poem I wrote was about the fireworks display on the last night of the Marshfield Fair.

4ᵗʰ OF JULY

Way high up
in dark summer skies

fiery flowers
bloom
BOOM
and die.

I liked writing poems. For one thing, a poem could be quite short: My Fourth of July poem contained just thirteen words! A poem only had to capture one thought or feeling.

I wrote other poems in school, including one about an ant and another about a bumblebee. When Mrs. Larsen passed back our poems I noticed that other kids had grades and comments on their papers, but there was nothing written on my bumblebee poem. After school I went up to her desk.

"You didn't write anything," I said.

"No, I didn't."

"What do you think?" I blurted. "I mean, is it any good?"

"It's fine." She gave me a long, thoughtful look. "But I think you could do better."

"Better? How?"

"I could be wrong," Mrs. Larsen said, speaking

slowly, "but when I read this poem, I got the feeling that you were mostly concentrating on the rhyme."

"I, ah, I don't know. Maybe."

"And on forming your letters correctly," she added.

It was true—every teacher I ever had complained about my sloppy penmanship. Mrs. Larsen leaned forward and smiled.

"Don't worry so much about making your poems rhyme, Ralph. And don't worry about your penmanship; I don't give a hoot about that."

I blinked. "You don't?"

"No, I don't. Just write what you feel. See if you can make your words fly."

For a long time, I thought about her words. Her advice made sense, but I didn't know how to apply it, or maybe I needed time to grow into it.

A week later Dexter Harris took us on another expedition to the marsh to dig for clams. Our appearance at the clam flat must have spooked a large blue heron because as soon as we arrived, it squawked and took off. I watched as it stayed low

The Bumble Bee

If unfortunately, I do not see,
In back of me
A big black Bumble Bee.

I am sure I will get the stinger
Although he is no great singer
He is very, very fast
And in a race is never last.

                                        Ralph Fletcher

over the water, pumping those big wings, struggling to gain altitude. My poetry sort of felt like that—flapping its wings with all its might, but having trouble taking off.

Mom with Johnny

November 22, 1963

M<small>R. NAGLE WAS MY</small> fifth-grade teacher. There were hardly any male teachers at South River Elementary School, so I felt lucky to have him, not that my other teachers had been so bad.

The school year got off to a smooth start. In October I went on two epic Boy Scout camping trips. We had beautiful fall weather, but by late November the weather turned cold. One Friday morning I went to school with a special feeling, like

I had extra money in my wallet. That's because my buddies and I had planned a huge football game—tackle, of course—at Steve Fishman's house after school. I couldn't wait for the game to begin.

Then something happened.

It was just before lunch. Mr. Nagle abruptly stood up and rapped a piece of chalk against the blackboard to get our attention.

"You're all going home," he announced. "Early dismissal."

Stunned silence.

"Wh-why?" Janet Anderson finally asked.

I'd never seen Mr. Nagle's face look so solemn. "You'll find out later."

"But—"

"No talking," he barked. "Gather your things. I'll lead you out to the buses."

Kids jumped up and descended on the coat closet, causing several minor collisions. I got caught in a confused tangle of lunch boxes, boots, jackets, and scarfs. I managed to locate my dark brown coat and grab it, but then I felt someone pulling it in the opposite direction.

"Hey!" It was Bobby Dane. "That's mine!"

We had a brief tug-of-war until I realized that Bobby was right. I'd taken the wrong coat.

"Sorry." I looked around until I finally found the right one.

We filed outside. All the grown-ups—teachers, bus drivers, parent volunteers—looked tense. Mr. Tobin, our principal, had his arms crossed stiffly, a stony expression on his face. He squinted fiercely, as if a great wind was blowing, though in fact the air felt eerily still.

When I got onto my bus I looked around for my brothers and sister, by habit. Jimmy, Lainie, and Tommy had already found seats. I watched Bobby, who was in first grade, trudge up the steps with a perplexed look on his face. Our driver, Ruben Gonsalves, shut the door, and the bus lurched forward.

"What the heck's going on?" Steve muttered.

"It's the president," Lainie said breathlessly from across the aisle. "Somebody shot him."

Steve and I stared at each other. "Shot the president? Who?"

"I don't know. Some guy."

"But he wasn't hurt too bad," added Sharon Oxner, Lainie's best friend. "The bullet just hit his pinkie finger."

I didn't argue with her, though that didn't make sense. Would they send all the students home from school because the president hurt his pinkie finger?

Mom was waiting at the bus stop. Other mothers—Mrs. Fishman, Mrs. Hunt—had gathered there too, which was highly unusual. We surrounded Mom, peppering her with questions.

"What's going on?" Jimmy demanded. "Why did they send us home early?"

"President Kennedy got shot," Mom said in her softest voice. "It happened in Dallas, Texas."

"But it was just his pinkie finger, right?" Sharon asked.

Mom shook her head. "It's worse than that, much worse. He got shot in the head."

Out of the corner of my eyes, I saw Steve spin away from his mother in disbelief.

"*What?*" he asked her. "*What?*"

"Is he . . . ?" Lainie murmured. "Is he going to be all right?"

"No," Mom said. Her lower lip trembled. "The president is dead."

"Really?"

Mom nodded.

Lainie gasped. Jimmy swore softly.

"Mom, Jimmy said a bad word!"

But Mom had already started walking away, and there was nothing to do but follow her. When we entered our house I could hear the TV in the living room. It was a newscaster, Walter Cronkite, explaining in a grave voice that President John F. Kennedy had been assassinated. It was a word I'd never heard before. Mom didn't watch TV during the day, but today she sat down on the couch, eyes glued to the screen.

"I'm hungry," Tommy said. "What's for lunch?"

Mom glanced over at Lainie. "There's bologna. Can you make some sandwiches?"

Lainie sighed. "Okay."

After we finished eating I ventured back into

the living room to sneak a look at Mom. Her face was very still. I followed one big tear as it moved slowly down her cheek. Bobby climbed onto the couch next to Mom. He tugged at her arm.

"Don't cry, Mommy."

"It's so sad," Mom whispered, wiping her face. "The president and his wife had two small children, just like Joey and Kathy."

"But it's not really real," Bobby tried to tell her. "It's just a TV show."

Jimmy snorted with disbelief. "Of course it's real!"

"No, it's not!"

"Yes, it is."

"Shush," Mom told them. "I'm trying to listen."

Ten minutes later the phone rang. Steve Fishman.

"My mom said we had to cancel the football game." He sounded frustrated. "Because of . . . you know."

Because of President Kennedy. Who had been assassinated.

At first that news felt like one of my not-quite-real daydreams. But seeing my mother cry reinforced the fact that something profoundly important had happened.

Dad came home from work and sat next to Mom. For the rest of the evening they never took their eyes off the television screen.

Today when I remember that fateful day in late November, it feels like looking through glass. Standing on this side of the glass, as an adult, I understand I was living through a historic moment that would forever change American history. (I would have a similar experience on September 11, 2001, when the World Trade Center burned to the ground.) And, having lost my own brother, Bob, I can empathize with the pain suffered by the Kennedy family.

But as a kid, standing on the other side of the glass, I was only dimly aware of the gravity of what had happened. In fifth grade I wasn't the least bit worried about death. I just wasn't. Death was something that happened to other people in faraway places like Dallas, Texas. I was surprised to see my mother cry, and I felt sorry for her, but I didn't experience John F. Kennedy's death as a personal loss. It may sound cold, but my overriding emotion at that time in my life was being bummed out that our epic football game had been canceled.

Little kids in Marshfield

Driving at Night

W₄ VISITED GRANDMA Annie and Aunt Mary in Arlington, Massachusetts, and drove home after dinner. It wasn't easy to squeeze everybody into the car. Lainie got the prized front seat, flanked by Dad and Mom. The middle seat overflowed with Jimmy, Tommy, and me. Plus I had the baby (Kathy) sitting on my lap. Bobby, Johnny, and Joey were jammed in the wayback, sitting cross-legged, facing backward.

Night fell. The combination of darkness, lights, and a belly full of Grandma's food made me drowsy. Soon the car became quiet and Mom started to sing.

I see the moon and the moon sees me
The moon sees somebody I'd like to see
Shine on the moon and shine on me
And shine on the somebody I'd like to see

Mom wanted us to sing along with her, so we did, though I would have been just as happy to stay silent and listen to her voice. I looked out the window, and sure enough, there was a moon peeping from between the tree branches.

Dad lit a cigarette. He opened the window a crack to let out the smoke, and in that second sleep entered the car. I could almost feel it. In my mind I pictured it as some kind of lazy snake, friendly and invisible, slithering in through the window. A moment later I felt it brush past my legs. Behind me I could hear the little kids talking with low voices.

The moon's following us. Look. No matter which way we turn, it's right behind us. . . .

"See the moon?" I whispered to Kathy.

No answer. Kathy's sweaty head had gone limp against my chest, and when I peeked around to look at her face, I saw that her eyes had closed. She was sound asleep.

Mom continued singing, working through her favorite songs: "Moon River." "Tammy's in Love." "The Wonder of You." She didn't have a strong voice, but she sang every word like it mattered.

No sound from the backseat. Swiveling around, I saw that those kids were dozing too. Three more gone! The sleep serpent continued moving around the car, silent, restless. One by one, every kid fell under the spell. I wondered who would be its next victim.

On the other side of the car I saw Jimmy leaning against the door, motionless. Then I realized that Mom had stopped singing—she was dozing too.

Dad and I were the last ones still awake.

The only noise I could hear was breathing, soft
and regular, like a lullaby you might hear someone
singing in the distance. That sound came from
every corner of the car. The car seemed to be filling
up with a sweet mist, which I thought must have
been baby dreams and little kid dreams and mother
dreams all mixed together. A mighty yawn tried to
rise up from deep in my throat, and it took all my
strength to swallow it down.

Dad snapped on the radio.

"Is the Red Sox game on?" I asked, piping up so
he'd know I was still awake.

"I think so," he said. "But I'll keep it turned
down low—go ahead and sleep."

"I'm not tired," I said, which wasn't entirely true.

Dad turned the dial. Moments later we heard
the familiar voice of Curt Gowdy, the Red Sox
announcer. His rich voice spilled into the dark inte-
rior of the car.

"The game is tied, four–four. Tony Conigliaro
steps to the plate."

Reaching back, my father handed me a piece of
gum, which I took and popped into my mouth. That

gum felt like a secret treat, something he could only give me because the other kids were sleeping. Chewing, I got that first flush of pure sweetness.

"I hope Tony smacks one," I said, using a quiet voice.

Dad nodded. "We could use a big hit right about now."

We faced straight ahead—my father in the front seat, me sitting behind—peering out into the night. Dad was the driver, so sleep wasn't an option for him. He absolutely had to stay awake. He was Ralph Joseph Fletcher, but I was Ralph Joseph Fletcher, Jr. As his oldest son, I decided it was my job to keep him awake, and I took that job seriously. I was determined to help him resist that sleep snake until we made it safely home.

Mom and Dad smoking

Smoking

SMOKING IS BAD news. Everybody knows that now, but when I was growing up people had a different attitude about it. Almost everybody smoked, and cigarette ads were all over the media. We watched TV commercials for Kent, Kool, Marlboro, and Lucky Strike. We hummed along to catchy jingles on the radio: *Winston tastes good like a cigarette should. . . .*

Both my parents smoked Pall Mall regulars,

unfiltered. Our house was filled with a thin gray haze. That was the atmosphere in which we lived and breathed, not bad or good, just there, like the nonstop sound of jabbering kids, or the ever-present smell of food cooking in the kitchen.

During art class, in school, every student had to make a papier-mâché ashtray. After the material dried and hardened, I carefully painted mine, wrapped it, and proudly presented it to Mom on her birthday. When my mother opened her present, she grinned and hugged me tightly against her blouse (which smelled like smoke).

Mom often smoked a cigarette while cleaning up the kitchen, but she especially liked to smoke while talking on the phone. When the phone rang, she'd pick it up—"Hi, Paulie!"—and cradle it between her shoulder and cheek, freeing her hands to unsheathe a cigarette. Surrounded by babies, toddlers, noisy kids, piles of laundry, and dirty dishes, my mother would talk and smoke, her eyes closed, leaning back against the wall. At those moments I imagined that the telephone cord and the smoke coiled together to form an umbilical cord, a lifeline that transported her to another, calmer world, at least for a little while.

Dad smoked almost everywhere: in the bathroom, in the car, and at the kitchen table after finishing a meal. I loved to watch him light his cigarette at the beach. He had a particular way of cupping a lit match against the wind as he brought it to the unlit cigarette held firmly between his lips. I thought his face never seemed so fierce, so concentrated and alive as it did when he lit a cigarette.

My father didn't stop smoking until he was almost sixty. We were proud of him for quitting, though by then the damage was already done. Fifteen years later he was diagnosed with lung disease.

"The chickens have come home to roost," he told me ruefully. "I should have never started smoking in the first place."

Tommy, Lainie, and Bobby

The Language
of Laughter

TOMMY AND BOBBY were goofing around on the back porch. Sitting at the kitchen table, I could hear their voices through the window screen. That noise was plenty distracting, but the kitchen felt stuffy and I didn't want to stop the cool breeze coming through the screen, so I left the window open and tried to block out their silly jibber-jabber. They were singing a made-up song:

Daisy, Daisy,
Long before the fashions came
With her head cut off and her belly too
She looked so much like a moooo . . .

That stupid song cracked them up when they
sang it, every time. I tried with all my might to
ignore them until suddenly they got seized by a fit
of helpless laughter. They couldn't stop laughing,
and didn't want to, either.

Was it really that funny? No, but for some fool
reason my brothers found it *hysterical.* Then the
sound changed. All at once my brothers stopped
using words but continued "talking" using nothing
but laughter. I made one last desperate attempt to
concentrate on my homework until I felt my mouth
twist into a reluctant grin.

So finally I put down my pencil and surrendered.
I closed my eyes and just let the sound of their laughter wash over me. And you know what? It was like
hearing any other noise from nature, like a couple
of songbirds calling back and forth at twilight, or a
wave thumping a beach followed by its echo. My

brothers hooted and cackled, first one and then the other, back and forth, back and forth, just like they were having a regular conversation. Honestly, it sounded like they were trading whole sentences of laughter. I wondered how you would diagram that kind of sentence, or if you ever could. It hit me that their laughter could be its own language like French or Spanish, one with its own rules and grammar and paragraphs and words . . . a secret language between blood brothers . . . and only they knew exactly what it meant.

Hearing them made me smile, but I felt a little wistful too. I was eager to grow up, to climb the ladder from childhood to adulthood. But some part of me wished I could join in my brothers' laughter, or return to a simpler time in my life when there was nothing better than spending an hour being silly like that.

Necco Wafers

All-Chocolate Necco Wafers

EVERY SUNDAY FOR weeks I stowed the two rolls of all-chocolate Necco Wafers in my lunch box. I wanted to show them to Gwen, but she still hadn't returned to Sunday school.

"Do you have any news about Gwen?" I asked Mrs. Wrenham.

She shook her head. "Sorry, I really don't."

One of the girls in my class also knew Gwen. She said she had heard vague rumors, an illness

137

of some sort, but she didn't have any hard information.

Then, a week after school ended, Mom motioned me into the kitchen.

"Did you know a girl named Gwen Givvens? Was she in your Sunday school class?"

"Yeah, why?" And why did she say *Did* instead of *Do* you know her? "What's going on?"

"Well . . . she died."

I froze. "Died?"

"Yes. It was in the newspaper. She had a brain tumor. That's very, very rare, but . . ." She studied my face. "Did you know her well? Was she a friend of yours?"

"No, not really." But I felt a pang of disloyalty in saying that. "Well, yeah, in a way. Sort of."

"Are you all right, Ralph?"

"Yeah." Though right then I couldn't make myself breathe.

"We can go to the funeral. I'd be happy to take you."

I shook my head. "No, that's okay."

Not sure what to do with myself, I wandered

through Ale's Woods. I found myself standing by the tallest tree there, an immense pine. On a whim I started climbing, and didn't stop till I'd made it all the way to the top. It was always a great feeling to be up high, high enough to gaze down at the tree-tops, though today I couldn't enjoy the view.

I thought about Gwen. I wasn't close to her like I was with Andy, Steve, and Freddy. There were several girls in school I felt closer to. But, still. I remembered the last time I saw her, when I said she looked nice in her red dress. I pictured her shy smile, the way her eyes crinkled when she looked at me. I wished I'd known that would be the last time I'd ever see her.

◆ ◆ ◆

The news about Gwen hit me hard, but I couldn't grieve. I didn't know how. The sadness stayed buried in a place deep inside me, remote and inaccessible.

A week later I bought a goldfish at a church fair. Honestly, I didn't even want a fish for a pet until I spotted those pathetic little creatures trying to swim in cramped, tightly sealed plastic bags. I felt so sorry for those fish I wanted to buy them all, but

Mom told me to pick one, so that's what I did. The man gave me a sheet of instructions for taking care of my fish. I followed those instructions to the letter, but the next morning I found my fish floating on the surface of the water, lifeless.

Dad gave my shoulder a sympathetic squeeze. "Too bad."

"Yeah." I felt dazed. "It happened so fast, I mean, I didn't even get around to naming the little critter. So . . . what should I do with it now?"

He cleared his throat. "Well, the traditional burial for a goldfish is flushing it down the toilet."

I shook my head. "I've got a better idea."

I wrapped the goldfish in a napkin and took it to the woods. I walked farther than I usually did. This time I went all the way to the Unexplored Territory, a place I'd never gone before.

I found a stream with lots of young white birches on both sides. Very peaceful. I dug a hole about six inches deep and placed the goldfish inside. But the moment I started to cover it with dirt, an idea popped into my head. I sprang up and ran all the way back to the house. In the top drawer of my dresser I dug out the two rolls of chocolate Neccos I'd been saving. I brought them back to the hole and placed them on either side of the goldfish.

I'd come to bury my dead goldfish, so why was Gwen Givvens the only thing I could think about? This felt way different from when President Kennedy got killed, way different. Gwen was the first person I'd actually known who had died. True, she wasn't exactly a friend, but she had gone out of her way to be nice to me. It felt horribly cruel and unfair that a sweet kid like her should get such a rotten deal.

I stared down at the rolls of candy. Necco Wafers had been our bond, a private joke between us. I remembered the day we told each other that chocolate wafers were our favorite. Nobody would have appreciated these rolls of chocolate Neccos more than Gwen. Nobody.

As I stared at the candy something shifted in my gut—a gush of tears started spilling out. It happened so fast I didn't have time to prepare myself.

I cried. I sobbed so hard my vision blurred and I couldn't see the goldfish or those rolls of Neccos or anything else in the world. In one way it was a relief, to finally let out my feelings. I felt glad to be in a far part of the woods with my own thoughts and tears as I crouched over that tiny grave.

Mom and Dad at the beach

Bird's Nest

A CATBIRD RETURNED to our house every spring.
We knew it was the same one by the peculiar notch
in its tail feathers. It had a regal look, a queenly bird
with smooth gray feathers until the sun hit them
and you saw a cool streak of blue.

Every year she (Dad insisted it was a female)
built a nest on the cherry tree in our backyard.
A few weeks later the male would show up. Those

catbirds were a sign of spring, and everyone looked
forward to their arrival. It made me feel special, or
honored, that these beautiful creatures chose to
spend the summer at our house.

One morning I watched the catbird fly to the
tree with a strand of grass in its beak. I kept my distance to avoid spooking it. Mom, Jimmy, and Joey
came outside and stood beside me, watching.

"What's she doing?" Joey wondered aloud.

Mom smiled. "Making a cozy nest where she
can lay her eggs."

"What's inside the eggs?" Joey asked innocently.

"Chocolate," Jimmy told him.

Joey's face lit up. "Really?"

Mom shot Jimmy a disapproving look. "Not
chocolate. Chicks. That's what they call baby birds.
She has to make a safe place for them to live and
grow until they're strong enough to fly." She rubbed
the top of Joey's head. "All moms do that."

◆ ◆ ◆

The following year we waited and waited for the
catbird, but it didn't show up. We started to get
worried.

"It's getting late," Lainie fretted. "It's already spring. She's running out of time!"

I should mention that there was a "family nest" in another part of our neighborhood that wasn't very peaceful. Months earlier, the McKenzies had moved into a house down the street. This young couple argued day and night. And they were loud! More than once I heard them yelling at each other when I walked past their house.

"What did you just say?"

"You heard me!"

"I asked you a question!"

"Why don't you get a job?"

Mom and Dad squabbled once in a while, but their arguments never got nasty like that. And they kept their voices low. The loud arguments between the McKenzies were shocking.

"They're going through a hard time," Mom said one night at supper, "but we should give them their privacy. It's none of our business."

"Then maybe they shouldn't broadcast their fights so the whole neighborhood can hear them," Jimmy muttered.

"Stay away from their house," Mom told him.

I mostly did stay away, though I have to admit their arguments fascinated me. A couple of times I deliberately chose a path that would take me to that side of the street, past the McKenzies' house, where I might hear a few choice tidbits from yet another fight.

Meanwhile, Lainie continued to worry about our missing catbird.

"What if it never comes back? What if it's dead?"

"It'll come back," I told her.

"Hey, I've got an idea," Tommy said. "Let's make a nest for her."

We stared at him. "Yeah, let's do it!"

We went to work. The little kids spread out to gather grass and thistle. Jimmy and I used our pocketknives to cut twigs that were tender and thin.

"How will we hold it all together?" Lainie wondered.

"That's a cinch," Jimmy said. He fetched a few handfuls of swamp mud, added a bit of water, and mixed it with the leaves, twigs, and thistle. This created a kind of dark, gluey mash. Working together, he and Lainie formed it into the shape of a nest. We all stood back to look at our creation.

I was impressed. "Looks pretty good."

Bobby nodded. "If I was a bird, I'd live there."

"Me too!" Joey put in. He started running around the yard, flapping his wings.

Jimmy climbed the tree and fitted the nest in the branches, placing it exactly where the bird had built its nest the previous year.

"How does it look?" he asked, jumping down.

"Perfect!" Tommy yelled.

Jimmy's hands were filthy, so he wiped his forehead with the back of his wrist. "It's still soft. The more it dries, the stronger it'll be. But if it rains . . . we're in trouble."

"It's not going to rain," Lainie declared, looking up at the sky. "It can't."

Meanwhile the McKenzies got their house painted, a nice shade of creamy yellow with brown trim. It looked terrific. I saw Mr. McKenzie in the front yard planting some bushes, whistling. That seemed like a good omen. Maybe things were getting better at their house.

One afternoon I saw Mom standing at the living room window. She looked sad.

"What's wrong?"

"The McKenzies are splitting up."

"Really?" I was shocked.

Solemnly Mom nodded. "I ran into Mrs. McKenzie at the supermarket. She started to cry when she told me, poor thing. She said they're getting a divorce. They're going to sell that lovely little house, and they just had it painted."

Next morning I was halfway through a bowl of Rice Krispies when Tommy came charging into the house.

"The catbird!" he cried.

We sprinted outside. There it was, perched on a branch in the cherry tree. I knew by the notched tail feathers that it was the catbird from last year.

Lainie shivered with anticipation. We all watched expectantly, eager to see what would happen when the catbird discovered the beautiful nest—a bird's idea of a dream house—we had built for it.

At first the bird ignored it. All of a sudden it

flitted over and peered inside. The bird tilted its head this way and that as if puzzled or confused.

"It's smiling," Lainie whispered.

"Birds don't smile," Jimmy told her.

"Look!"

The catbird reached forward, removed a piece of grass from the nest, and tossed it away. Then it grabbed a twig that was clotted with dried mud, and dropped it onto the ground.

"Wh-what's it doing?" Tommy sputtered.

"It's . . . it's wrecking the nest!" Lainie cried.

We watched in horror as the catbird dismantled the nest we had so carefully made for it. Mom came out to see.

"She's messing up the nest we made!" Tommy yelled. "She's blowing it up!"

"My goodness," Mom murmured.

Bobby looked worried. "What about the baby birds? Where will they live? If they don't have a nest, they'll fall out of the tree."

"You watch," Jimmy told him. "I bet you ten bucks she builds her own nest, just like she did last year. I guess she doesn't trust anybody to make it for her."

Mom folded her arms. "Maybe there's a lesson in this. Birds have to build their own nests, piece by piece. Nobody can build one for them."

She gave me a meaningful look, and it dawned on me that Mom didn't just mean the catbird. She was talking about the McKenzies too.

That was one of the perks of being an "in-betweener"—getting a special dose of Mom's wisdom—grown-up ideas the little kids wouldn't understand or maybe weren't ready for. It made me feel special when she shared those things with me.

Mom, Grandma Annie, and Dad
at Mom's graduation

On the Back of
the Bus

RUBEN GONSALVES WAS the small, wiry, smoke-skinned man who worked the fields in the farms around us. Word had it that he came from the trop-ics, maybe Honduras or Panama, though nobody knew for sure. He was a familiar sight in our neigh-borhood, wearing a straw hat to keep out the sun as he rode a tractor. The man was a gifted farmer. No wonder people were eager to hire him to work their fields.

"Run over to Ruben's field and pick five ears of corn," my mother often said. "I'll pay him later."

Everybody called it *Ruben's field*, even though he didn't own the land. We ran over, knowing Ruben wouldn't mind, knowing you couldn't find any corn anywhere that was fresher or more delicious.

Ruben never said very much, though he performed one feat that made him a legend among the neighborhood kids.

"Eat a worm, Ruben!" we begged when we saw him working in the field.

If you were lucky, he would obligingly pick one up—not a little one, either—strip away the dirt with one hand, pop the wriggling creature in his mouth, and start to chew.

"Mmmm," he'd say, smacking his lips.

I had seen this routine several times, so I knew what to expect; still, I always stood there, dumbstruck, while Ruben munched a big old earthworm.

Ruben worked several different jobs, including driving the school bus. His son Mark, who was my age, would usually be the only kid on the bus when it rumbled up to our stop at 7:55 in the morning.

One fateful day I sat next to Mark in the backseat. Our bus was about half full, with another bus directly behind us. As we were driving along, Mark made some kind of gesture to the other driver. I was half asleep at that time in the morning, so I didn't see what motion he made, whether it was friendly or rude, or possibly misunderstood. At any rate, the other driver took offense and angrily beeped his horn. Ruben had to pull our bus to the side of the road and shut off the engine.

Moments later the other driver got out of his bus and climbed onto ours. The guy came barreling down the aisle. He grabbed Mark Gonsalves by the back of his shirt and dragged him off the bus. The other kids and I rushed to the right side of the bus to watch what would happen next. Through the windows we saw the driver yelling at Mark Gonsalves, with Ruben standing a few feet away.

Suddenly—*WHAP!*—the driver slapped Mark hard across the face, causing his head to snap back.

Ruben stood there, working his mouth, but said nothing.

Then it was over. The driver stomped back to his bus. Mark climbed onto our bus and took his seat next to me. Ruben started up the engine and we lurched forward, continuing the regular route to school.

Out of consideration for Mark, I kept my eyes forward. After a few minutes, I stole a glance at him. He wasn't crying, though his expression held a mixture of frustration and rage. I wondered whom he was most angry at—the other driver for hitting him or his father for not trying to stop it.

All this time my fists stayed clenched; later I would find a row of indentations where my fingernails had left marks on the palms of my hands. I knew I had just witnessed something terribly wrong, but I didn't know what to do about it. I felt ashamed at my own helplessness.

This happened in 1964, before the civil rights movement really took hold in the United States. Marshfield was a white town. Ruben and Mark Gonsalves were the only people of color I knew.

Many times I have thought back on what happened that day, and wondered if that driver would have dared to slap Mark Gonsalves in the face, with his father watching helplessly, but for the color of their skin.

Tommy

A Conflict of
Interest

By sixth grade, most kids my age no longer
considered it "cool" to be in Boy Scouts. Some kids
in school teased me if they saw me in my uniform.
I felt torn. I still loved scouting: I mean, what could
be better than sleeping under the stars? Or roast-
ing meat over an open fire beside a noisy stream?

But more and more I was drawn to other things.
They had a series of school dances on Friday nights,
which often fell on the same night as a Boy Scout

camping trip. One night we camped in a torrential rainstorm; the rain was so loud against our tent I couldn't sleep. It was cozy and dry in the tent, but I kept picturing my classmates at the dance and wishing I could be with them.

A few weeks later we went on a two-day camp-out in the Catskill Mountains. The trip got off to a good start. The first afternoon we set up our tents and prepared to cook our evening meal. Patrol leaders sent out younger Scouts to forage for firewood. Soon you could smell and see the cheery sight of a half dozen campfires burning all around the campsite. Then a loud sound ripped through the air.

RAT-TAT-TAT-TAT-TAT-TAT-TAT-TAT-TAT-TAT-TAT-TAT!

What a commotion! It sounded like somebody firing a machine gun. I ran in the direction of the noise with Mr. Briggs following close behind.

"What's going on?" he demanded.

Ricky Topham, the patrol leader, was all shook up. "Somebody threw a string of firecrackers into our fire!"

"What?!"

"Any idea who did it?"

He shook his head. "Nope."

"Talk to your patrol," Mr. Briggs instructed Ricky. He turned to his other patrol leaders: Andy, Steve, and me. "Keep your eyes peeled, all of you."

"Who would do something that dangerous?" Steve wondered aloud.

"I don't know," Mr. Briggs murmured. "But I'm ninety-nine percent sure it was someone in our troop."

The incident with the exploding firecrackers made everyone jumpy; it took a long while before the group finally calmed down. We climbed into our sleeping bags and slept through the night.

The next day we had a five-mile hike planned so we got up early.

"You don't need to make a big fire for breakfast," Mr. Briggs reminded us. "A small fire is easier to put out."

I had just assigned two kids in my patrol to help me make breakfast when—*RAT-TAT-TAT-TAT-TAT-TAT-TAT-TAT-TAT-TAT-TAT-TAT!*

Another uproar. More firecrackers!

"What's going on?"

"What the—"

"Quiet!" It was rare for Mr. Briggs to raise his voice; everyone fell silent.

"Fall in over here!" he ordered. "Make a line!"

"But . . . we're just about to have breakfast," one kid said.

"Breakfast can wait!" Mr. Briggs snapped.

We all lined up. Under different circumstances, it would have been comical to see this ragtag line of kids, half dressed, standing at attention in the early morning light.

"Patrol leaders!" Mr. Briggs cried.

Andy, Steve, Ricky, and I all stepped forward. Mr. Briggs gathered us in a circle.

"You know these kids better than I do," he said quietly. "I want you to go up and down the line and find out who you think did this. It must stop."

We walked up and down the line, studying the

boys' faces. Gary Fishman, Timmy Ross, Tombo Hunt, my brother Jimmy. Finally I found myself standing in front of my brother Tommy.

There it was—a telltale twitch in one corner of his mouth.

My eyes narrowed. My expression grew hard. Panic sprouted in his eyes.

Because he knew that I knew that he had done it.

His eyes met mine. *Please, Ralphie,* they pleaded. *Don't turn me in. Please please please.*

Usually I found it easy to choose between right and wrong. But this time it felt more complicated. Throwing firecrackers into the fire wasn't just some silly prank. Somebody could have gotten seriously hurt. As patrol leader, I knew that it was my responsibility (that word again) to find out who had done it. Mr. Briggs was counting on me to do exactly that. And I knew he would mete out swift punishment. Mom and Dad would get a phone call to come pick up Tommy immediately. Who knew, Mr. Briggs might even kick him out of the troop.

What should I do?

"Patrol leaders!" Mr. Briggs snapped, motioning us back to him. "Well? Any idea who did it?"

"No," Andy mumbled.

Steve and Ricky shook their heads.

"C'mon, guys," Mr. Briggs said impatiently. "Give me something. Ralph?"

I swallowed. Until that moment, I honestly didn't know what I would say.

"I don't know," I managed.

He looked at me closely. "No idea?"

"No."

Mr. Briggs turned to the line of Scouts. "All right, listen up! I don't know who did this, but it's going to STOP NOW. Understand? If there is one more firecracker incident, I will cancel the rest of the campout and we'll all go home. Is that crystal clear?"

Kids nodded.

"Finish your breakfast," Mr. Briggs barked. "We'll start the hike in thirty minutes, and I expect everybody to be ready."

The line broke and kids headed back to their campsites. I could feel Tommy's eyes on me, so I motioned for him to follow. We ducked behind a line of scrub pine trees.

"Thanks for not busting me," he whispered. It was pathetic to see the relief on his face.

"I should have, you know," I hissed. "What the hell is wrong with you?"

"I shouldn't have done that," he said earnestly. "I'm sorry."

I stared at him in disbelief. "You're sorry? That's all you can say?"

"I don't know . . ." He looked genuinely perplexed.

I grabbed his arm, hard. "Do you have any more firecrackers?"

He hesitated, which told me that he did.

"You bring me whatever you've got left," I ordered. "If you don't bring those firecrackers in five minutes, I swear I'll turn you in. I don't care if you're my brother."

"I promise," he said.

"Don't promise. Just do it."

I was furious with him, not just for his behavior but for putting me in a position where I had to go against what I knew was right. Tommy was guilty, but I couldn't throw my brother to the wolves. I just couldn't. He was my blood, and I felt a primal urge to protect him . . . even from the consequences of his own actions.

Bobby, Grandma Annie, and me
at our house in Winnetka

Moving

AT DINNER ONE night, Dad theatrically cleared his throat.

"We're moving to Winnetka, Illinois," he announced. "It's near Chicago."

Stunned silence.

"Your father got a promotion," Mom added cheerfully. That was her role—trying to put a positive spin on not-so-wonderful news. "We'll be able to afford a bigger house with one more bathroom."

"I'm happy to hear that," Lainie said, though she didn't look happy. None of us did.

"Chicago?" I muttered. "Does that mean I have to start rooting for the White Sox? Because that's NEVER going to happen."

Dad smiled. "Not if you don't want to. Anyway, I think I may have found a nice house."

I couldn't believe my ears. "You've already been house-hunting?"

"I have."

"Does it have a swimming pool?" Tommy asked.

"No swimming pool," Dad said, "but it's a terrific place."

"Are there woods in the back, like here?" Jimmy wanted to know.

Dad nodded. "There are definitely trees in the yard."

Jimmy snorted, like he couldn't be bought off that easily.

"Trees in the yard isn't the same as a forest," Jimmy pointed out. "Not even close."

"When are we gonna move?" Tommy asked.

"July fifteenth," Dad told him.

Moving. It didn't seem real. The word felt like something nasty I'd eaten but couldn't digest, so it just sat there, rock-heavy, in the pit of my stomach. I figured telling my friends might help the news sink in, so that's what I decided to do.

We met in my backyard, in the clearing, between two of the gigantic tripods Jimmy had designed. The tripods had been constructed using long pine logs lashed together using special knots only he knew how to tie. We'd built those tripods under his direction over a year ago, and they were still holding up. I realized they would be here longer than I would.

"When?" Andy demanded.

"July fifteenth." I'd already looked at a calendar—in the exact middle of the summer.

For a long moment nobody said anything.

"Dad says we'll come back to visit next summer," I added.

Freddy cracked his knuckles. "Everybody says that, but it never happens. When you move, you're gone—period."

Steve glared at him. "That's a little harsh."

Freddy shrugged his big shoulders. "Yeah, well."

I stared at him. It *was* harsh, but I suspected it was probably true.

◆ ◆ ◆

Over the next few weeks Mom got boxes and started packing our stuff. The real estate agent showed people our house. Still, the news didn't sink in. I continued living day after day, feeling as if I'd be in Marshfield forever, even though my brain kept trying to remind me, *This will end soon. Soon you'll be gone, and this place will be nothing but memories.*

One night I had trouble falling asleep. Listening to the Red Sox game on my transistor radio didn't help. I kept thinking about my Marshfield friends. Was Freddy right? After we moved to Chicago would I ever see them again?

Dad came into the room and sat down on the edge of my bed. "You know how you guys do fun-sies and keepsies when you play marbles?"

"Yeah," I replied.

"Well, grown-ups do something like that too."

I sat up. "What are you talking about?"

"Remember when I said we were moving? That was funsies—not keepsies."

I stared at him in disbelief. "You mean . . ."

"It was a joke!" He grinned and spread his hands, as if releasing a spray of invisible confetti. "We're not moving from Marshfield. Are you kidding? We're not going anywhere!"

I got a surge of intense Christmas-morning elation. Not moving! It was the ultimate practical joke. He and Mom had been yanking our chains all along. Not keepsies—only funsies! Though it did seem awfully strange to hear those words come out of my father's mouth.

That's when I woke up. Dream over.

Lunch with kids from the neighborhood

The Other
Fletchers

SAYING GOOD-BYE TO Andy, Steve, and Freddy
would be the hardest thing I'd ever had to do. But it
wasn't just my friends I'd miss. I realized I'd also
miss their toys, their zany little brothers and sisters,
their dogs and cats. I'd miss the smell of their houses,
so different from my own. I'd miss their fathers and
especially their mothers: Mrs. Hunt, Mrs. Fishman,
and Mrs. Fletcher.

The Fletchers lived down the street. They weren't

related to us, though we had a lot in common. We had eight kids; they had ten, so Acorn Street was crawling with Fletcher kids. There was a saying on the street where I lived: Either you were a Fletcher or you pretended you were one.

The other Fletchers were older than us. Freddy Fletcher's parents were ten years older than mine, so most of his brothers and sisters were older. Freddy was the third-youngest kid in the family. Some of his big brothers and sisters were already in their late twenties or early thirties.

Sometimes we'd have a friendly argument as to which house was best—Steve Fishman's or Freddy Fletcher's. (Andy and I accepted the fact that our houses, while perfectly nice, were not in the running.) Steve's house and Freddy's house both had fantastic chicken coops, barns, under-barns, root cellars, storage bins, and workshops that were perfect for our games of War and Hide-and-Seek. Which place was best? It might have been a tie, though Freddy's house was located next to the golf course, so we found lots of lost balls in the woods, which tipped the balance in his favor, though just barely.

Freddy's house was huge, sprawling, and O-L-D. I'm talking ancient, *historic*. The structure had been built in the 1690s! After centuries of family life, one side of the house had settled; the kitchen floor was definitely tilted in one direction. You could feel it when you walked in. If you dropped a marble on the left side of the room, it would roll downhill and smack against the wall on the right.

The Fletchers' kitchen always had a pungent smell of sweet molasses. That's because Freddy's mother made big batches of molasses cookies. She didn't bake cookies once in a while or just on a holiday. Nope—she baked molasses cookies every morning. And they were out-of-this-world delicious. She made enough cookies for all ten of her kids, and her kids' friends too. One day I went into the kitchen where dozens of molasses cookies were cooling on the counter.

"Help yourself, Ralphie." Millie gave me a teasing smile. "You're a Fletcher, aren't you? You never have to ask—you're family. Take as many as you want."

Like I said, we weren't related, but Millie seemed

to enjoy this little joke between us. But she didn't treat me any different from other neighborhood kids on account of my last name. Andy and Steve had the same privileges. They could also grab molasses cookies whenever they wanted.

Millie Fletcher was important to me. I knew I would miss her a lot when we moved away from Marshfield. I wasn't one of her kids, but she cared for me as if I was. She was like a second mother. She always included me when she brought out Popsicle treats, or glasses of lemonade, or a big tray of watermelon slices. If they decided to go to the beach while I happened to be at their house, she'd take me along with them. If I got hurt, or cut my knee, Millie would carefully patch me up so I was good as new. Afterward she'd wipe my tears, give me a reassuring hug, and kiss the top of my sweaty head. It felt like a real mother's love—pure and unconditional—even if we weren't connected by blood.

Johnny

The Earthworm

Moving day crept closer and closer. Mom told us to sort through the stuff in our bedrooms and put aside what we didn't need; she would donate it to Catholic charities. Meanwhile she continued packing boxes, stacking them in the corners of the house.

One day we got some shocking news—a family had bought our house. The Leatherbees. I actually met one of the kids, a boy named Rob about my age. Rob Leatherbee seemed okay, though it felt weird to imagine him living in MY house, the house where I grew up. I tried not to think about it. I continued living my life as if everything was normal, which was crazy, because I knew that our ship had hit an iceberg and was taking on water, fast.

One Saturday morning Andy came over. His father wanted help digging up some bushes. We worked on the far side of Andy's house. I spaded deep into the black earth, but when I lifted my shovel I saw that I had accidentally cut a worm in half. I felt horrible.

"Sorry!" I said to nobody in particular.

"It's okay," Andy assured me. "If you cut a worm in half, both sides will grow into a new worm."

"Well, not quite," Mr. Hunt corrected him. "It's true that the half that has the worm's heart will grow back its body and live. But the other half, the half without the heart, will die."

That idea haunted me. That evening I opened my notebook, hoping that writing might help sort out my jumbled thoughts.

My life feels like that earthworm I mistakenly cut in half. Part of me will get left behind . . . the

176

other part will go to Winnetka. The half with the heart will live, but what about the half without a heart? Will that part wither and die? I don't want that to happen. I don't want either half to die.

I shut off my light and closed my eyes. The faces of my friends materialized before me: Andy, Steve, Freddy. I realized that in the past few weeks we had spent little time talking about my moving away. I wondered why. Maybe if we'd been girls it would have been different, but my buddies and I never talked about serious stuff. I guess we couldn't find the words, or maybe we knew they'd be too painful if we ever did speak them out loud.

Next morning I was wandering in the backyard when I noticed a grown-up standing near the swamp. Mom. That was unusual; my parents rarely ventured into the woods.

"What are you doing?" I asked.

"Admiring the swamp cabbage," she said, pointing.

I wrinkled my nose. "Quite a smell."

"I'll say. Do you remember the time Bobby brought me the white flower of a swamp cabbage on my birthday? That flower stunk to the high heavens." She smiled. "You guys all poked fun at him, but that was really quite sweet."

I nodded. "It's the thought that counts, right?"

She smiled but then she turned away from me, and I realized she wasn't laughing anymore.

"Mom?" I whispered. "Are you okay?"

She sniffled, and wiped her eyes with the back of her hand.

"Moving is hard for you kids, but it's hard for me too," she said in a hoarse whisper. "So many memories. Marshfield has been a great home for all of us."

"Yeah." I didn't dare try to say any more than that—I was afraid I'd start bawling. Instead I put my hand on her shoulder and gave her a little squeeze.

✦ ✦ ✦

Finally the big day arrived. Jimmy said good-bye to Ricky Topham and Timmy Ross. Lainie said good-bye to Sharon Oxner. Tommy said good-bye to Michael Fletcher and Gary Fishman. Bobby said good-bye to Paul Fishman. I wanted to say good-bye to Andy, Steve, and Freddy Fletcher, but they weren't around. I suspected they wanted to avoid the melodrama of a final farewell. I didn't hold it against them.

Over the years I had found a number of arrow-heads around our neighborhood. I loved knowing that Native Americans had roamed the same forests where my friends and I played. I opened a shoe box and selected the four best specimens from my arrowhead collection—one for each of my friends, and one for me. I brought those arrowheads to a place in Ale's Woods and buried them under six inches of dirt.

As I was repacking the dirt, I spotted a fat earth-worm. It reminded me of what Mr. Hunt had said a few days earlier about what happens when a worm gets cut in half. *The half that has the worm's heart will grow back its body and live. But the other half, the half without the heart, will die.* I had been trou-bled by this idea, but not any longer. I realized that my Marshfield memories would never die. They would take root, and grow, and always have a central place in my heart. Always.

Back home I was eating a second bowl of cereal

when the doorbell rang. When I opened the door, I was greeted by my friends.

"C'mon, Ralph. We're taking you to the woods one last time."

I had to talk Dad into it, since we would be leaving later that morning. Finally he let me go with them. How could he not? I followed them into Ale's Woods, feeling happy and suddenly carefree, like things would work out somehow, even if I couldn't say how. They led me into the woods along a path I knew by heart. That forest *was* my heart.

"What's going on?" I asked.

"We're having a funeral," Andy replied.

"For who?"

"You," Steve explained.

"A funeral! Hey, I'm moving. I'm not going to be dead!"

"You'll be dead to us."

We walked past the spot where I had buried the four arrowheads a few hours earlier. I considered mentioning it to my buddies, but I decided not to. It seemed right that those arrowheads should stay buried in Ale's Woods, along with all my other memories of Marshfield. I had left them in a secret part of the forest, but I knew where to find them. I still do.

A few minutes later I was lying down, playing dead, while my friends had a little ceremony to recognize that I would be leaving them. They stood on both sides of me—the closest friends I had on planet Earth—and told stories about what I meant to them. It was like a final eulogy, I guess. The whole thing was sad, funny, a little weird, and very sweet. I was all choked up and couldn't speak. Thankfully, I didn't have to do anything but lie there, listen, and take it all in. I felt very lucky in a Tom Sawyer–ish way. I knew then that I would remember these friends for the rest of my life. We kept in touch with letters after I moved away, and many of us still keep in touch today.

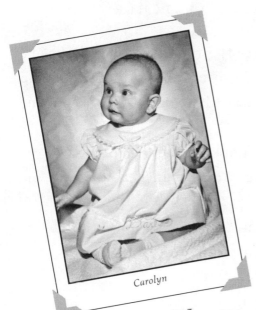

Carolyn

The Final Fletcher

M Y LITTLE SISTER Kathy was baby number eight. She was the final Fletcher. Or so we thought.

We spent the next three years living in Winnetka, Illinois. After that, we moved to West Islip, a town on the south shore of Long Island, New York. I was a senior in high school. I had a cool job digging clams on the Great South Bay, working for myself on a small boat that Jimmy and I bought with our own money. I had several close friends, plus my first (sort-of) girlfriend. Best of all, I had a driver's license. So things in my life were going swimmingly when Mom pulled me aside one afternoon.

"Ralphie, can I talk to you for a minute?"

The serious expression on her face gave me pause.

"What's wrong?"

"Nothing." But she looked pensive.

"What is it?"

"I'm three months pregnant."

I blinked at her.

"No way!"

"Way," she said wearily. "Big way."

"But, you're, uh . . ." I didn't know how to finish the sentence.

"I'm no spring chicken," she admitted. "I'm forty-three years old. It's not technically too old to have a baby, but . . ."

Mom stood five foot two inches. I was pushing six feet, so I towered over her as we spoke. Often when I looked at her I had the same thought—what a miracle that all of me had come from her. I thought she was still beautiful, though years of nonstop mothering had definitely taken a toll on her. I was seventeen, Jimmy was sixteen, Lainie was fifteen, Tommy was fourteen, and Bobby was thirteen (born in the same year)! She had five teenagers in the house, plus three younger kids, and now another one on the way. No wonder she looked careworn.

"So what do you think?" she asked nervously. "You'll be eighteen by the time the baby's born. Will that feel strange?"

"No, I think it's great," I assured her. "The more the merrier."

She sighed. "That's easy for you to say."

The other kids were equally thrilled, though we did have a squabble about whether it would be a boy or a girl.

"If it's a boy, that would make seven brothers," Tommy pointed out. "Seven is a lucky number."

"Seven brothers would be an abomination," Lainie countered. "I'm praying for a little sister."

"Me too!" Kathy put in.

Jimmy smirked. "Yeah, well, keep praying."

Six months later, on May 6, 1971, we were eating supper when Mom suddenly sat up straight.

"My water just broke," she announced.

"The amniotic fluid," Lainie explained, in case we didn't understand.

Dad drove Mom to the hospital. I stayed behind and played my familiar role, making sure younger kids did their homework and got to bed on time. In many ways I was still an in-betweener—half kid, half parent. By now, playing that role was baked into my identity.

Next morning a shrill cry yanked me from a deep sleep.

"It's a girl! It's a girl!"

It was Lainie, calling up from the first floor.

"It's a GIRL!"

"Wh-what?" I looked over at Jimmy, sleeping on the other bed. "What did she say?"

"It's a girl!" Lainie yelled triumphantly. "G-I-R-L!"

After a few days, Dad brought Mom and the baby home from the hospital. After he put a pillow on a chair in the living room, Mom gingerly sat down. We all crowded around, eager to get a closer look. The baby had a red scrunched-up face and was fast asleep. I thought she looked exhausted, like she had just completed a baby's version of a marathon race.

"What do you think?" Dad asked, nudging Jimmy.

Jimmy nodded, noncommittal. "Well, it's a baby, all right."

"A *female* baby," Lainie said with a satisfied smile.

"I think she's adorable!" Johnny cooed.

"I expect you guys to all pitch in more around here and help your mother," Dad said. "Babies take a lot of work."

"When can I play with her?" Kathy asked.

Mom smiled. "Not for a little while yet."

"What's her name?"

"Carolyn."

Carolyn. To my ears the name sounded like *caroling*, the joyful singing we did around Christmas time. That seemed appropriate. I was singing inside. We all were.

"Nine kids is an uneven number," Jimmy pointed out. "It's unbalanced. You know, Mom, maybe you and Dad should go for a nice round number: ten."

Mom gave him the Look. "Don't even joke about that."

I leaned forward and inhaled the sweet baby smell. Bobby touched the baby's nose. Lainie caressed the baby's tiny cheek with the back of her hand.

I looked at Mom. I felt close to everyone in my family, for sure, but *close* doesn't even begin to describe the way I felt about Mom.

She gave me life.

She taught me how to love.

She was the first woman I ever loved.

Often, I believed I knew what Mom was thinking. Like right now. With the whole family crowded around, oohing and ahhing over this tiny new life, she must have been thinking, *Freeze this moment when our family is happy and healthy and whole. Don't let it end.*

Me and Bobby clamming

Epilogue

MY FAMILY DIDN'T have much to complain about in 1971. The eternal Fletcher baby—along with diapers, tiny socks, rubber nipples, baby spoons—had made a triumphant return. Now we had enough kids to field an entire baseball team! Nine is a lot of mouths to feed, but Dad had received a big promotion, so our fridge was full. We lived in a lovely house on the south shore of Long Island, New York.

I had gotten accepted at a top-notch college. A happy ending, right?

Well, not exactly. A few years later, in 1974, a dark cloud swept in and cast a terrible shadow over my family. In the spring of that year, Jimmy (nineteen) got in a car wreck in Iowa; it nearly claimed his life. A few months later, Joey (thirteen) got seriously burned when he tried to take some hot oil off the kitchen stove. He spent five weeks in the hospital. A month later, Bobby (seventeen) was in a head-on collision in West Islip, New York. He clung to life by a thread, and everyone prayed like crazy, but a week later his heart gave out and he died.

In writing this book, I decided not to focus on that part of my life, partly because I already talked about it (in the "Bobby" chapter) in *Marshfield Dreams*. This collection of stories focuses on those years when I felt like an in-betweener in the family, when I was trying to figure out who I was.

Bobby's death was a cataclysmic event for me and my family. We were damaged. Yes, we would heal, but only to a point. Some part of the Fletcher family would always be missing. After we lost

Bobby, my life would forever be divided into Before and After.

An event like that pokes a hole in your world, like a wormhole or a black hole in space. It distorts time. In some strange way, Bobby's death casts a dark light back on the innocent Marshfield years that came before. Today it feels as though that tragedy, or at least its seed, was part of me even when I was a little kid.

Wouldn't it be great if you could go back in time and weed out all the bad stuff in your life . . . cherry-pick only the happy memories? But it doesn't work that way. All of life's experiences—the bad as well as the good—make up who we are. I am shaped by every story in this book, all the people who touched me and influenced my life. Even the ones who are gone.

Except they're not gone, not really. I hold their spirits inside me. Keep them close to my heart.